MW01145539

GOD KNOWS

how to raise your kids...
(even if you don't!)

JOE MCGEE

God Knows How To Raise Your Kids: Even If You Don't
Updated Edition 2014
ISBN 978-0-9903045-0-0

Copyright © 1998, 2014
Joe McGee Ministries, Inc.
Stonebluff Publishing House
P O Box 680446
Franklin, TN 37068

Cover Design: Hampton Creative, Inc.
Editor of Updated Edition: Linda Schantz

DEDICATION

To my wife Denise, the love of my life,
who inspires me to be a better father.

And to Sarah, Jessica, Corrie, Tessa, Lauren, and John –
our reward from God.
Thank you for who you are and for what you have become.

A special thank you to my multi-talented editor, Linda Schantz,
whose expertise and patience made this book possible.

What People Are Saying About This Book

Joe McGee delivers some of the most entertaining, yet practical and insightful teaching on the family available today. Your family will never be the same after reading this book!

— Pastor David Blunt
Church On The Rock, St. Peters, MO

Joe can pack more into one sermon or one book than anyone I have ever met. His insights into biblical parenting are unique and will open up scriptural secrets and common sense applications which will powerfully change your family. Don't miss the message of this book.

— Reverend Bob Yandian
Bob Yandian Ministries, Tulsa, OK

This book helps remind me of how to handle some of the daily challenges of parenting, as well as, how patience and prayer are key elements in effective parenting. This book is full of ways to keep your sanity in the challenging world of parenting.

— Jayni

I can't speak highly enough of this book! A must-read for every parent. It changed how I parent and opened my eyes to so much!!! Even though the book is about parenting there are so many nuggets of wisdom about so many other areas of life! It is full of God's Word and so applicable to every phase and situation of parenting. I'm so thankful to Joe for writing this!

— Melissa

I have read a lot of parenting books in my time and this is the best yet! The Holy Spirit has surely led Joe McGee in writing this wonderful book. The principles (straight from God's Word) make so much sense and are such an encouragement.

— Shannon

I love it! It is a great book. Very helpful!

— Cara

TABLE OF CONTENTS

FOREWORD

Dear Parents,

Here it is! Joe McGee has written a book to help you raise good Christian kids. And he's qualified! He's not only a gifted teacher and public speaker, he's a great dad. He and his family are part of our church and he has lived the things he shares in *GOD KNOWS HOW TO RAISE YOUR KIDS... EVEN IF YOU DON'T!*

If you are really serious about raising your children to become disciples of Jesus Christ, you'll enjoy these teachings. Joe shoots straight from the hip and tells it like it is, but his message is soaked with compassion. You will gain new confidence in your role as a parent and find courage to steer your kids in the right direction – even when they offer resistance.

Your children are worth the time and the effort it takes to train them right. You won't have another chance, so let Joe McGee help you get it right. He knows what he's talking about.

— Pastor Willie George
Church On The Move
Tulsa, Oklahoma

INTRODUCTION

Kids Were A God Idea

From conception, to birth, to becoming an adult, children will spend almost a third of their lives under the care of their parents. Training and teaching them is a full-time job.

There is no such thing as a perfect child because there is no such thing as a perfect parent. And yet, there are strong children and there are strong parents.

There is no greater responsibility and no greater privilege than raising the next generation. The Book of Psalms says:

> Children are a gift from the Lord; they are a reward from Him
> Psalm 127:3 NLT

The first time someone quoted that to me I thought, *That's a lie! Somebody who has no kids wrote that!*

I had six kids and I didn't see a rewarding thing about it. Don't get me wrong, we love our kids. We wanted a big family. But what reward? They cost money from the time they arrive and up until, and even after, they leave. They chew the corners off the end table, need braces on their crooked teeth, outgrow their clothes, eat you out of house and home, flush things they shouldn't and don't flush things they should. I thought, *God if that is your idea of a reward, go reward my neighbor for a while. You've rewarded me enough!*

However, children are a reward.

Children Are A Reward

The writer of Proverbs knew the joy that comes to the parents of well-trained children and the grief which comes to those whose children have not accepted training and discipline.

A wise son maketh a glad father: but a foolish son is the heaviness of his mother.

Proverbs 10:1

Children are a reward, but there are two lists of rewards given in Proverbs. Children can bring you sorrow, grief, bitterness, shame, and hatred.

They can also bring you joy, gladness, happiness, peace of mind, and be a delight to our souls.

Students are not greater than their teacher. But the student who is fully trained will become like the teacher.

Luke 6:40 NLT

That makes the home the center of education for children.

Successful Children Is The Goal

- Parents who **fear the Lord, will have successful children** (Psalm 112:1-2).

- Parents are to **train up their children** in the way they should go (Proverbs 22:6).

- Parents are to **teach the Word** of God diligently to their children (Deuteronomy 6:6-7).

- **Children who are taught** the Word of God **will have great peace** (Isaiah 54:13).

- **Children are to obey and honor their parents,** so their lives will go well and they will live a long time (Ephesians 6:1-3).

- **Parents are not to provoke their children to anger** by the way they treat them and should not over correct them (Ephesians 6:4).

- **Parents are to bring them up with the discipline and instruction** from the Lord, with the sort of education and counsel the Lord approves of (Ephesians 6:4).

- Children are to always **obey their parents, for this pleases the Lord** (Colossians 3:20).
- **Parents are not to aggravate their children** or they will become discouraged (Colossians 3:21).

Parents Are To:

Fear God

Train

Teach

Not provoke

Discipline

Instruct

Children Are To:

Live in peace

Obey

Honor

Please the Lord

Passing On The Faith

Abraham was chosen as the father of our faith because God knew he would teach his children and his grandchildren (Genesis 18:19).

President Abraham Lincoln wrote:

"A child is a person who is going to carry on what you have started. He is going to sit where you are sitting and, when you are gone, attend to those things which you think are important. You may adopt all the policies you please, but how they will be carried out depends on him. He will assume control of your cities, states and nations. He is going to move in and take over your churches, schools, universities and corporations. All your books are going to be judged, praised or condemned by him. The

fate of humanity is in his hands. So it might be well to pay him some attention."

Throughout the Bible God puts great emphasis on the next generation.

- God commanded the children of Israel to **teach their children to the fifth generation** (their great-great-great grandchildren) that they might have hope in God and not forget his great works and goodness (Psalm 78:1-9).
- A good man **leaves an inheritance** to his children and his grandchildren (Proverbs 13:22).
- Children were not to lay up for the parents, but the **parents were to lay up for the children** (2 Corinthians 12:14).

Our children are facing issues previous generations never had to face. Life has gotten busy. But God has not left us alone. He promised He would never leave us or forsake us and that our children would be successful everywhere. Using God's blueprint we can launch the greatest generation in the history of the world.

After spending thirty years working with families and raising six great kids, we have found that *God Knows How To Raise Our Kids ... Even If We Don't.*

We hope you enjoy this practical, humorous, Biblical study on parenting.

CHAPTER 1
Biblical Parenting

For many years parents have tried to raise their children based on what they saw others doing and what they learned by reading articles from magazines or online. Some may have had a measure of success, but the answers that bring long-term solutions are found only in the Word of God. These answers are there for those who will seek them out.

Many years ago when working in church as a children's minister, I discovered that, for some reason, parents considered that the answer for raising godly children was the church. They thought if they could just get their children to church, somehow their kids would turn into spiritual giants. So every Sunday morning those children were sent off to church after having consumed and experienced God knows what throughout the previous week.

When I began my life as a parent, the only thing I knew about parenting was to tell children what not to do. As I had always heard it said, "You just can't tell children what not to do fast enough."

But I thought there just had to be more to parenting than saying no all the time. That's no fun; children don't like it, and neither do parents. Moms and dads can get hoarse from yelling at their kids so much, with their veins standing out and blood pressure rising.

There just had to be a better way. I thought, *I refuse to live the way we've been living. We have to find a change somehow.*

"Teach Us About Parenting"

I remember one day years ago talking to my pastor, saying: "Pastor, we have to find somebody to teach us young pups how to parent. With two toddlers right now, I don't know whether we're coming or going, and I don't see things getting any better in the future."

"That's a good idea, Joe. You need to find somebody, I guess."

"Well, I'll start looking," I said.

I spent the next two months hunting for someone at our church who would be willing to teach a class on parenting. But no one would do it. The answer was always the same: "I can't teach a class on parenting; I'm too busy working on my own children. Ask me again in ten years; maybe by then I'll know something."

> **You just can't tell children what not to do fast enough!**

Then I started looking for somebody with white hair. I thought anybody who had white hair was bound to have learned the ropes on parenting (assuming, of course, that person wasn't just prematurely gray!).

When I asked one lady about teaching the class, she looked at me and said, "Son, my baby is 45 years old and I'm still working on him! I don't know anything about parenting."

At the end of those two months, I could see it was a fruitless endeavor, so I went back to the pastor and said, "Pastor, this is a hopeless situation. It's obvious that nobody feels qualified. Now I know why we're in trouble."

Then he said, "Joe, you're just going to have to do it yourself."

"Well, I don't feel qualified either," I said, "but I'll give it a go." So I sat down with my wife, Denise, and we talked about things we wanted to know as parents. We wrote down a list of 48 subjects for us to contemplate as topics in a class.

The first subject I wanted to consider was the question, *Where do babies come from?* (That was, in fact, the topic of our first class.) Other subjects that we listed for possible discussion were thumbsucking, bedwetting, making good grades in school, lying, sex, dating, making friends and the biblical discipline of children.

Class Begins

When we held this class for the first time, seventeen people showed up. We met at our church every Sunday for an hour before the evening service started. I would teach for about fifteen minutes; then we would talk with one another about that subject.

There were three tools I used in dealing with every topic: a Bible, a concordance and a book about that subject, which we would buy at a Christian bookstore. In preparing for the class, I wrote down every scripture I could find about that particular subject.

Encouraging parents to use pencil and paper to take notes during the class, we began to build. We would briefly share at the beginning of class what the world was saying and doing about our subject, based on information we gathered from newspapers, books, magazines and the media. Then we would find out what God had to say in His Word and share information from good Christian books on the subject. What God had to say was usually the opposite of everything we had ever heard or read from the world's point of view.

Our turnout for the class varied depending on which subject we were discussing. When we had classes on how parents were to teach their children about sex, I would have to bring in extra chairs. When I taught a class on child abuse, hardly anyone showed up. Other subjects covered were how to teach children about handling money and about picking their friends.

Called Into Full-Time Ministry

About once a month somebody would call and say, "I know someone at your church, and I've heard about your teaching. Would you come to our church and teach us on parenting?"

So we began traveling around to other churches. Then God separated us out into full-time ministry.

Now, as the parent of six children, I've always been a homebody. When I'm at home, I like to shut the gate and go into the house. So I was concerned, wondering, *How can I travel around the country teaching other parents about parenting, if I'm never able to spend time at home with my own family?*

To be honest, I'm home much more now than I ever was before. When I was a school administrator, it seemed I was never at home. I worked in the same building where my children attended classes, but I never saw them. I am able to see my family much more than before. Although my kids are all grown, they still travel with me some of the time, and some of them work at our office.

Family Background

Let me give you a little information about our background. My wife, Denise, and I were childhood sweethearts. When you've found something good, there's no need to shop around, so we got married.

Both sets of our parents came from big families. There were twelve brothers and sisters in my father's family, five in my mother's, twelve in my father-in-law's family and six in my mother-in-law's.

So when our parents got married, they'd had enough of big families, sharing everything from biscuits to pillows to clothes. My parents decided they only wanted one boy and one girl – and that's what they had, my sister and me. Denise's dad and mom had two boys and a girl.

But Denise and I grew up going to those big family reunions, and we both liked that. When we got married, we wanted a big family; in fact, we wanted five children. We decided to wait five years before beginning our family, and we did.

We asked God for five children, but since the Bible says in Ephesians 3:20 that God does above and beyond all we could ask or think, we got six! We ended up with five daughters and a son. Our last child was the boy.

Every Child Is Different

It's amazing how different children can be. About the time I thought I had learned how to raise our firstborn, she grew into another stage. It seemed I could never quite catch her. Then our second girl came along. By then I thought I'd learned all about being a parent, but our second daughter was nothing like our first.

When I was disciplining, I could give one of those ugly-face looks. (You know, something that looks like Attila the Hun raised from the dead.) When I looked at my firstborn that way, she responded immediately. But when I tried using that look on my second born, it came back to me good measure, pressed down, shaken together and running over. Dealing with her required a different approach.

That's true with every child. Each one is a little different.

Dwelling Together In Unity

Take six children and two adults, each having their own unique set of gifts and personalities; put them all under one roof and have them dwell together in unity. That is the miracle we call family.

It took work, and lots of it. Knowing that the devil's main tactic is to divide and conquer, we still keep a constant vigil to make sure we don't let him in.

A classic example of how quickly things could get out of hand was the simple task of getting everyone ready to go to church.

It usually started when I went to shave in the morning only to find my can of shaving cream empty because my toddler used its entire contents the night before to take a bubble bath. After finding a new can, I'd finally lather up. Then I took my razor and, with one quick swipe down my face, I would nick myself in three different places. The reason: a dull razor! Several of the women in our house had used my razor to shave their legs. After stopping the bleeding, I'd reach for my toothbrush only to find it had been knocked from its holder and was laying on the floor behind the toilet.

About this time I learned we had a typical math problem: too many women and not enough pantyhose! That required a stop on the way to church at the convenience store to pay twice the price for each pair. As the father of five daughters, I truly believe it's better to buy pantyhose by the pound than by the pair!

When we got everyone out of the house and into the Suburban, we suddenly remembered that our vehicle was totally trashed during Saturday's all-day excursion to ball games, birthday parties, the grocery store and a trip to the vet.

By the time we finally got to church, we needed to sing praises to God.

But in those rare and precious moments when things were quiet and settled, we would all admit that we wouldn't trade this life for anything else in the world.

Practical Parenting

In this book, we'll deal with many practical things in the study of biblical parenting. But you need to realize there is no such thing as "seven methods" or "four ways" or "three keys" to parenting.

Basically, there are two areas you need to understand and deal with in parenting:

1. **Attitude**
2. **Relationship**

You have to get your attitudes and your relationships down pat. The rest is not that big of a deal. But you can only attain the right attitudes and relationships by being a doer of the Word of God (James 1:22).

There's a key scripture, on which we will base this entire study on parenting. In describing the boy Jesus, **Luke 2:52** says: **"And Jesus increased in *wisdom* and *stature*, and in *favour with God and man.*"**

> **There's no such thing as "seven methods" or "four ways" or "three keys" to parenting.**

This verse could be said another way: *Jesus increased mentally, physically, spiritually and socially.* When any of these four areas are out of line in our lives, we will be faced with challenges.

I don't think God left us down here on earth just to hang on, but having talked with so many parents across the country, I've heard them say, "We're just waiting for our children to turn eighteen and move out of the house."

We need to realize that things will not automatically get better when our kids turn eighteen. We won't retire from parenting when that occurs; we will still be their parents when they get to be 58. If things aren't going well now, and they won't automatically get better in the future, we need an attitude change.

Let's look again at Luke 2:52: **"And Jesus increased in wisdom and stature, and in favour with God and man."**

I believe God is very specific and detailed in His instructions. This scripture gives us four areas in which Jesus developed in His life on earth. They are: *wisdom, stature, favor with God,* and *favor with man*.

Let me give you four more common words we would use today for these areas:

1. **Wisdom** = *Vision*
2. **Stature** = *Discipline*
3. **Favor with God** = *Stewardship*
4. **Favor with man** = *Friendship*

In the following chapters we'll examine each of these subjects in relationship to our children, describing ways in which they can grow and develop the same way Jesus did.

CHAPTER 2

Wisdom = Vision

And Jesus increased in wisdom and stature, and in favour
with God and man.

Luke 2:52

The first subject in this verse of scripture is *wisdom*. It says:

And Jesus increased in *wisdom*....

The word I will use for *wisdom* is *vision*. Jesus had a vision for His
life.

The Bible says Jesus only did what He saw the Father do and He
only said what He heard the Father say (John 5:19; 14:10). Jesus
knew where He came from. He knew why He was here. And He
knew where He was going. He asked His parents in Luke 2:49,
"Don't you know I need to be about my Father's business?" He
laid down His glory in Heaven and took the form of a servant.
(Philippians 2:7). Hebrews 12:2 says He endured the Cross for the
joy that was set before Him. He had a purpose for coming to earth.

Children Frustrated With Life

Over the years, most of the family counseling problems I have dealt with involved kids. These days so many children have no idea why they're here or where they're going, and they seem bored and frustrated with life.

These children are classic examples of the life described in Psalm 1:1. This scripture says:

> Blessed is the man that walketh not in the counsel of the ungodly, nor standeth in the way of sinners, nor sitteth in the seat of the scornful.

If our children are not walking with God, they are walking in the counsel of the ungodly, following the advice and plans of the ungodly. After a while, they will begin standing in the way of sinners, meaning they will be hanging around sinners and submitting to their lead. Then after that, they will sit down in the seat of the scornful, resting and relaxing in a life of sin, complaining about everything and everybody.

> **These days so many children are bored and frustrated with life.**

After listening to a person for only five minutes, you can usually mark him, because what's in his heart will come out of his mouth. As Jesus said, **"Out of the abundance of the heart the mouth speaketh"** (Matthew 12:34).

Many children are just frustrated with life. They say "Life's a bum deal, and I've been dealt a bum hand." But that's a lie of the devil. The world is always trying to paint that idea in our children's minds. To them the grass is always greener on the other side of the fence.

Without godly wisdom and a vision for life, children will progressively settle for the world's lies and become dissatisfied with everyone and everything around them.

Walking In Wisdom

Wisdom has several attributes, but let me just hit the high points for you. Let's look first in Proverbs 3:13-15.

> Happy is the man that findeth wisdom, and the man that getteth understanding.
>
> For the merchandise of it is better than the merchandise of silver, and the gain thereof than fine gold.
>
> She is more precious than rubies: and all the things thou canst desire are not to be compared unto her.

Then according to verse 16, if we are walking in wisdom, the benefits are excellent. It says:

> Length of days is in her right hand; and in her left hand riches and honour.

With wisdom, three benefits will come to us while we are here on this earth:

1. **We will live a long life.**
2. **We will have honor.**
3. **We will have wealth and riches.**

Without wisdom, we will never have these three.

According to Proverbs 9:10, we can't have wisdom unless we have the fear of God. This verse says, **"The fear of the Lord is the beginning of wisdom."**

If our children have no fear of God, they will have no wisdom, but they need wisdom to experience long life, honor, wealth and riches. Without wisdom they will struggle through life.

We can do a lot of good things for our children: We can send them to the best schools, buy them the most expensive tennis shoes and sign them up to play on the best Little League baseball teams. But their lives will still be miserable if they don't have wisdom.

Every person is born with certain God-given gifts and talents. As Scripture says, **"The gifts and calling of God are without repentance"** (Romans 11:29). Your gift will make room for you; it can even make money for you. But if you have no wisdom, your life will be miserable. True wisdom comes from the Word of God.

So, Jesus increased in wisdom. In other words, *He had vision.* Vision is important. As Proverbs 29:18 says: **"Where there is no vision, the people perish."**

Put God's Vision In Your Child's Heart

I want to paint a broad picture of vision in your mind.

As a parent (whether single or married; it makes no difference) our number-one job is to place God's vision in our child's heart. The world won't do it. Our neighbors won't do it. The school system won't do it. As parents, we have to plant that vision within our child. We have to paint a picture in his heart of how God sees him. Proverbs 23:7 says, "As a man thinks in his heart, so is he."

In other translations Proverbs 29:18 reads like this:

"Where there is no vision, the people dwell aimlessly."

"Where there is no vision, the people dwell carelessly."

"Where there is no vision, the people dwell in violence."

People who have no vision can get bent out of shape about life. They can beat up anyone who stands in their way: their husband or wife, their children, their relatives, their neighbors. These people want to fight against anything that moves; they're just mad about life!

You've heard the classic excuse before: *"I didn't ask to be born!"* (Maybe you've even said it.)

No one ever asked to be born. Life is like riding on a roller coaster. You'd better pull back the bar in your seat and hang on, because, whether you asked for it or not, you're going on a ride through life that's filled with ups and downs.

Jesus had vision. He knew why He came and where He was going. Many children these days don't have any idea about their future. It's up to us as parents to plant a picture about God in our child's heart to help them navigate the ups and downs of life. But how are we to do that?

Suppose every morning the world came to your house, knocked on your door and said: "We represent your state and your county. We're here just to let you know we want to be a blessing to your children. We plan to speak good words to them and bring good things into their lives for the rest of their days."

That would be wonderful!

But it will never happen in this world! The devil is at work in the world, trying to take complete control over our children.

A Parent's Responsibilities

According to Romans 13:1-8, every person in a position of authority – and that includes a parent – has two responsibilities: to confront and punish that which is evil, and to praise that which is good.

This means as parents we are to confront that which is wrong in our children and teach them to repent. Then we are to praise that which is good in them.

It's our responsibility as moms and dads to be the number-one cheerleaders in our families. Nobody else will cheer our children on the way we can.

I have to admit, praise doesn't come naturally to me, so I have to work at it. I hate to admit it, but criticism does come easy. I could get up every morning and see plenty of things to get bent out of shape about. I don't have to look hard; those things are usually staring me in the face. Sometimes I had to really work at finding things in my kids to praise.

God Designed Praise

God is the One who created praise. According to Scripture, there are some strange creatures hanging around His throne in Heaven just to praise Him. In the book of Revelation, it says these creatures have one job day and night. They cry out, **"Holy, holy, holy, Lord God Almighty, which was, and is, and is to come"** (Revelation 4:8).

Suppose someone walked up to God's throne and said to Him, "Say, Father, what's with all these strange creatures all around here?"

"I made them to praise Me."

"Is that all they do?"

"Yes."

"Don't they ever take a break?"

"No."

"Are you going to let them stop after a few thousand years?"

"No, they'll be praising Me forever."

"Don't they ever get tired?"

"No, they just keep praising Me."

It sounds good, doesn't it?

Well, we are made in God's image (Genesis 1:27). That means if God needs praise, we need it, too.

Our Children Need Our Praise

Children are definitely seeking praise. They need to receive praise from their parents. Without it, they will seek after praise from their peers for all the wrong things they do. They'll find praise somehow and somewhere. If righteous praise doesn't come from their parents, children will get unrighteous praise from some other source.

When we're doing our job as parents, our children are not nearly as likely to be swayed by peer pressure. But we have to work at it. I have to purpose in my heart that I'm going to do righteously by affirming my children with the Word of God.

We must constantly reaffirm within our children the vision that God has for them. Like Abraham, we are to call those things that be not as though they were (Romans 4:17). If our kids are weak, we must say they are strong. We have to speak what God says in His Word.

> **It's our responsibility as moms and dads to be the number-one cheerleaders in our families.**

Training Is Vital To Success In Life

> Train up a child in the way he should go: and when he is old, he will not depart from it.
>
> Proverbs 22:6

We will be looking into this scripture in greater detail, but first let me point out one important fact.

As this verse says, we are supposed to *train up our children*; but, if we're not careful, instead of training them, we'll simply raise them.

We give them their own rooms, their own cars and iPods, and leave them to plan their own lives. Then we wonder why they don't turn out any better. Training involves having a specific end result in mind. Training is showing our children what to do and then seeing to it that they do it.

Training is vital to success in life. Let me give a couple of examples.

When I went away to Army basic training, I was placed under the authority of a drill sergeant. I was taken away from my parents, my girlfriend, my chocolate donuts and my TV. All the hair was removed from my head, my civilian clothes were taken away and I was dressed in a green uniform. Then I was put in a room with 120 other guys. I had to get up at crazy hours and couldn't go to bed when I wanted to. I was in training. But the more training I received and the quicker I was able to perform, the sooner I began to enjoy some freedoms. Training was vital to my success.

I also remember an experience my dad had trying to raise tomato plants. He raised some of the most delicious tomatoes in the Tennessee Valley. But that wasn't always so. In the beginning he wasn't very good at it.

A little bud would come up on the vine, and a nice tomato would be ripening. But when Dad went out to pick it, the vine would be laying over on the ground under the weight of the tomato – and the worms had beaten him to it!

Then one day an elderly neighbor came by and said, "Mr. McGee, you need to train those plants. We'll get some wire mesh and put some around them." When he came back later, he pulled out the old plants and put up the wire mesh. Then Dad started all over again with some new plants.

When the plants began to bud and little tomatoes came out, the pressure of the green tomatoes began to pull the plant over to one side. So Dad took some twine, tied it around the stem and mesh and gently pulled the plant back in line. When pressure drew it the other way, he pulled it back in the opposite direction. He kept straightening the neck of that little stem until he could grow tomato plants four feet tall and was producing fruitful crops. Those tomatoes could be eaten because the plants had been trained to grow and produce.

During the time of training, parents can get an idea of where the end is, but the problem is that they usually don't stay focused on the end. They're always looking at right now, saying, "Things aren't good now and I'm mad." Parents need to be thinking about the end result. Remember, God calls those things that be not as though they were (Romans 4:17).

Most drivers' training manuals will tell you that the best way to stay straight while driving on the highway is not to look directly across the front hood of your car but to look at a fixed point down the road. Keep your eyes looking ahead toward where you want to go, not just at where you currently are.

God Sees The End Result

When the Angel of the Lord came down from Heaven seeking Gideon, He said to Gideon, **"The Lord is with thee, thou mighty man of valour"** (Judges 6:12).

Gideon's response shows us that he didn't see himself that way. Gideon was a man without a vision. He saw himself as weak, poor and unable to do anything about his situation. He looked up as if to say: "Angel, you must have made a wrong turn coming out of Heaven. My name is Gideon. I'm the youngest member of my family, and we're the poorest of our tribe. The Lord has left us and we've been taken captive. Things are hopeless and the people here are all afraid and starving to death." (Author's paraphrase; see vv. 13, 15.)

But the Lord's response reveals how He saw Gideon by faith: **"Surely I will be with thee, and thou shalt smite the Midianites as one man"** (Judges 6:16).

God did not call Gideon what he was. By Gideon's own admission, he was a wimp hiding in a hole. **God called him what he was going to become.**

God doesn't see what we are. He sees what we will become. That's how we, as parents, are to see our children. I don't look at my children for what they are. Right now they may be klutzy. I see them, not for what they are, but for what they will become.

In the gospel of Luke the Bible talks about how Jesus stayed up all night praying, talking to the Father. He was getting ready to select the twelve men He would name as apostles (Luke 6:12-16).

Jesus only did what He heard the Father say, so I can imagine the conversation going something like this:

> **God doesn't see what we are. He sees what we will become.**

"Okay, Father, who are We going to pick as My disciples?"

"The first one will be James."

"Oh, that's good, Father. I like James. He's a good, solid businessman. Who's next?"

"I want you to pick Matthew."

Jesus thinks a minute, then says, "There are lots of Matthews. Which one do you mean?"

"You know the one."

"Oh, Father, You don't mean that tax collector, do You?"

"That's the one."

"But, Father, I can't have a tax collector following Me. I mean, things are bad enough with the ministry as it is. People like that are hated and spit upon."

"Take Matthew."

So Jesus says, "Not My will, but Thy will be done." After writing down the names of James and Matthew, He asks, "Who's next?"

"I want you to pick Peter."

Jesus thinks a minute, then says, "But, Father, there are several guys named Peter. Which one do you have in mind?"

"You know the one."

"But, Father, he has a hot temper. I can't have him following Me around in the ministry."

"Pick Peter."

Again, Jesus says, "Not My will, but Thy will be done," and He adds Peter's name to the list.

The twelve apostles were some of the klutziest guys ever put together at one time.

Using New Testament street talk, Jesus once said to them: "How long do I have to put up with you guys? When are you going to get some faith? I can't hang around here forever. I have to go home! You need to get hold of this" (Author's paraphrase; Mark 9:19; 4:40).

Then two of the disciples, James and John, who were called the sons of thunder (Mark 3:17), brought their mother to Jesus to get permission for them to sit on either side of Him in glory. They seemed more concerned about titles and positions than about the ministry. (See Matthew 20:20-21.)

But these twelve messed up guys are the same ones God used in three and a half years to turn the world upside down. They worked at evangelizing the whole known world.

So, as parents we must have patience with our sometimes klutzy kids. God looks at things differently than we do. Looking down through time, He sees the end result. He doesn't call us what we are – but what we will become.

CHAPTER 3

Painting The Vision

Let's consider the stories of Joseph and Daniel, two of my favorite Bible characters. Their parents had planted some truth inside them, and they had a vision of who they were and what they were to do.

Both Joseph and Daniel ended up in foreign countries under the leadership of unbelievers. They were people from the wrong culture who spoke the wrong language and practiced the wrong religion. In these strange lands, they had no family, no friends and no finances. Yet both of them were given great authority over the heathen nations.

Do you know what was said about Daniel under King Darius? Scripture says, **"... An excellent spirit was in him; and the king thought to set him over the whole realm"** (Daniel 6:3). Darius, being a heathen, didn't know God and didn't care to know Him. But he saw something special in Daniel; he just didn't know what it was. Yes, there was something special about Daniel: it was the Spirit of Almighty God at work in his life!

There were three different kings, one after the other, who had run that country, and Daniel sat under their regimes. Each of those kings saw the good job Daniel could do, so Daniel was put in a position of authority and kept in charge.

This kind of promotion can take place in our children's lives, too. With the Spirit of God inside them, they can walk out into the world and be blessed as they follow God's plan and purpose for their lives.

That's what I want for my children. I want them to achieve everything God has for them, whether living under my roof or going out into the world. Wherever they are, I want God to look at them and speak those beautiful words: **"Well done, thou good and faithful servant."** (See Matthew 25:20-21.)

A Godly Seed

In dealing with children, no two of them are the same. As stated in Psalm 127:3, **our children are a reward from God.**

God isn't just looking for seed. He's looking for godly seed.

But, Mom and Dad, you'll never hear from the world that children are a reward from God. Instead, you'll read how they cost you so much money and take up so much of your time.

Throughout the book of Proverbs, there are two lists of rewards that having children will bring to us. One list is positive and one is negative. Our children can bring us blessing, honor, peace and prosperity; or they can bring grief, sorrow, shame and dishonor.

"Which reward am I going to get, God?"

"This is entirely dependent upon you, Son."

According to the book of Malachi, **God isn't just looking for seed. He's looking for** *godly* **seed** (Malachi 2:15).

Take my word for it: Having six kids doesn't make you holy. It can drive you insane or keep you broke if you don't know and do the Word of God.

If you read the Bible, you'll see that there were times when God specifically got involved in children being born; but it was rare. Some people never married; others were married but never had kids. Some got married and had only one child, while others had twelve or more.

Sometimes God was very detailed, telling certain people that they would have x-number of kids. But 99 percent of the time, God was saying to His people: "When you sow human seed, you'll reap human crop. You can have as many children as you want. **There will be plenty of children and plenty to feed them; I have never seen the righteous forsaken nor their seed begging bread."** (See Deuteronomy 28:11; Psalm 37:25.)

My Seed Shall Be Mighty

One of the required courses at our school, called "Biblical World View," involved the students selecting a single subject of their choosing, which could range anywhere from politics to sports.

Each class period, the students cut at least one article out of the daily newspaper to be kept in a scrapbook about the topic. At the end of each nine weeks, they condensed those forty-five articles into a one-page summary report. Then they were given one week, using a Bible, a concordance and a dictionary, to find a minimum of twenty-five scriptures also about that subject, condensing them into a one-page summary report. They then had to give a five-minute oral report comparing the two summaries.

The purpose? To show that, regardless of what subject they picked, whatever the world had been saying about that subject for the last nine weeks, God had been saying almost the exact opposite for thousands of years.

One student had picked the subject of overpopulation and had cut out articles about how we were running out of food, water, oil and land, as well as, how the ozone layer around the earth is being depleted. Yet in his research of the Scriptures, he discovered in Revelation 20:6 that there will be at least a thousand-year reign of our Lord Jesus Christ on this *existing* planet – not a new planet. Meaning that, unless we've missed the Rapture of the Church, when Jesus comes to take us to be with Him in Heaven, there must be at least a thousand-year supply of food, water, gasoline and ozone on this planet.

Now it's a fact that humans are abusing this planet. That's what sin does; it abuses. But even with all the abuse that occurs, there are still plenty of supplies left.

I love to say about my children what God's Word says in Psalm 112. (You have to choose what you're going to believe for yourself. Don't look to your neighbors or your friends; look to God's Word.)

> Praise ye the Lord. Blessed is the man that feareth the Lord, that delighteth greatly in his commandments.
>
> *His seed shall be mighty upon earth:* the generation of the upright shall be blessed.
>
> Psalm 112:1-2

"Big deal," some would say. "Maybe each of your children will find a good godly spouse, but they'll have to work two or three jobs between them just to live. With so much inflation, a normal house will cost half a million dollars."

"I don't care if houses cost two million dollars," I would answer. "If I fear God and delight in His commandments, blessings will come to my children. Psalm 112:3 says, they'll have wealth and riches in their house."

"Okay, so what if your kids do get wealthy?" some might continue. "Marriages today fall apart."

"Yes, it can happen," I would answer. "But God is the great Redeemer and Restorer."

Psalm 112:4 says, **"Unto the upright there ariseth light in the darkness…."** If we'll just hang tough and stand on His Word, God promises to show up on our behalf.

> **If we'll just hang tough and stand on His Word, God promises to show up on our behalf.**

How Big God Is

Sometimes we don't think God is big enough to do anything for us, but let me tell you how big He really is.

My kids always took part in the science fair at our school, which was an eventful time of the year. While they were working on their projects, our house was turned into a trash heap for about seven days, and it looked like a tornado had run through it. It was a hectic time of year, but we survived it.

My older daughter was interested in astronomy, so during her project we were studying the sun, the planets and their moons. I discovered just how amazing our universe is. It's a big place!

Through the use of the Hubble Space Telescope, we are able to see things we didn't even know existed. There are hundreds of billions of galaxies in the universe, and we live in one of them, the Milky Way, which is among the smallest of all those galaxies. If you go out at night, you can look up and see the Milky Way. The galaxies are hundreds of thousands of light years apart.

There are some 200 to 400 billion suns in our galaxy alone. The sun in our solar system is one of those, and the earth is more than a million times smaller than our sun.

When I was growing up, I had a tough time trying to figure out what God looked like.

I remember asking my dad such questions as: "What does God look like? Does He have a long beard and white hair? What does He do all day long? Does He ever get bored?"

"No, Son, God isn't bored; He's just there. Remember He told Moses, 'I AM THAT I AM.'"

I heard Dad say that to me, but it didn't really register. Then I asked him, "Well, when was God born?"

"He wasn't born, Son; He just is."

"But everybody has to be born, Dad. We have to start somewhere."

"No, Son, God never started."

Once I read an article about the space shuttle. The author noted: "We are very pleased with the space shuttle program, except for one thing: We wish we could design it to achieve the speed of light. If it could travel the speed of light, we could do some long-range space exploration."

Scientists have speculated that at the speed of light (186,000 miles per second) time would cease to exist in space. On a space mission traveling at that speed, an astronaut could take forty years going out and forty years coming back. When back on the earth, he wouldn't have aged while the people here would be eighty years older.

Let me give you an idea of how fast that is. Let's say you point a .22 rifle into the air and pull the trigger. If that bullet traveled at the speed of light – 186,000 miles per second – it would have circled the earth seven times before you even took your finger off the trigger.

Now, lining this up with the Word of God, the Bible says that God is Light (1 John 1:5). That's why there is no time in Heaven; everything just is.

My dad, who was a real character, always had to be on time. He was always looking at his watch, saying, "What's the schedule? What time is it? Where are we going?"

So after he went home to be with the Lord, the kids were saying: "Can you just imagine Grandpa getting up this morning in Heaven? He doesn't have a watch, so that's driving him nuts. He must be rubbing his wrist raw, thinking, *What are we doing today?*"

Let's suppose there was a conversation between two people in Heaven. Can you imagine it going something like this?

"How long have you been here?"

"Oh, about a thousand years."

"Well, I've only been here 22 days. I'm just getting used to the place."

No, people in Heaven are not aware of time. Heaven has no concept of time – no sun, no moon, no yesterday, no tomorrow. I would call Heaven an "is" place.

Now let me tie all of this together to help you realize how big God is.

In our own galaxy, the Milky Way, it's 100,000 light years from one side of it to the other.

Let's say, for example, I could get into my pickup truck, leave this earth and cruise up into space. If I kicked it into high gear, traveling at 186,000 miles per second, it would still take me 100,000 years to go from one side of our galaxy to the other. And our galaxy is one of the smallest!

How big is space? Our brain could never comprehend it. We can't even think of it. It's big – even bigger than Texas! And it took no effort at all for God to create it; He is even bigger than that!

How Small God Is

Now let's consider the science of DNA. There's been much talk in recent years about the use of DNA in catching criminals.

At the moment of conception, when the sperm and egg come together, the first thing that's created is a fertilized egg cell, in which is found a little twisted chain of molecules of DNA. It's like a little guy with a clipboard who writes down a description of all the cells in the body. It's called the body's blueprint. It would be his job to tell each cell what they are to do as they come into existence. He says to them: "I want you two million cells to line up over here. You, four million, go there. You twenty-two need to be here, and you five should go over there."

> Our kids must learn how big God is yet how small He can become to reach them where they are.

Everything about our physical anatomy is planned out at the moment of conception. Our hair color, our eye color, our nose size, how knobby our knees are – all of it can be found in our DNA.

God, the Creator, went into that much detail in creating our physical bodies, going down to even the minutest of molecules as a basis to form the entire human being. God put us on this tiny planet engulfed in a universe so big that a super-computer would burn out trying to cover it all.

God Has Big Plans For His Kids

Did God, Who made us and placed us in a universe so large we cannot conceive of its limitless size and in a body which, at its conception, was blueprinted down to the smallest detail, leave us here in between to run around like a rat in a maze in this thing called life?

If that were true, He might have said, "Well, I got them started. Now I'll see how they make it. Oops! There they go bumping into things."

No, God didn't leave us here on our own.

The Bible says **the steps of a righteous man are ordered of the Lord** (Psalm 37:23). Nobody else, except you and I, as parents, are better qualified to plant inside our children the vision of how big God is and how small He can become to reach them right where they are.

Remember, God called to the apostle John on the isle of Patmos and said to him, **"... Come up hither, and I will shew thee things which must be hereafter"** (Revelation 4:1). Then John was taken up into Heaven and shown things of the future.

Imagine it: God is sitting at the center of existence where there is no time; and in our universe, time revolves around Him. Where we are, time is; where God is, there is no time.

God told John to watch while future events were taking place. As John wrote down all that he saw, he must have been thinking, *Wow! That's really something!* The things he saw hadn't happened yet; but he was seeing them as they were occurring.

Don't miss that last point: All that John saw hadn't happened yet; but he was watching as those events were taking place before him.

That's why Jesus, speaking of the Holy Spirit, said: **"Howbeit when he, the Spirit of truth, is come ... he will shew you things to come"** (John 16:13). Why? Because, He is God.

God knows what we're going to do two minutes from now, two days from now, two months from now and two years from now. God has good plans for His children.

When Israel was taken captive by Babylon, God said to them: "Boys, I know it doesn't look good, but this wasn't My plan. **The plans I have for you aren't meant to harm you but to prosper you. I have plans to give you a future and a hope."** (Author's paraphrase; see Jeremiah 29:11-14.)

You need to realize that the world is lying when it says, "God did that to you!" God didn't do it! The devil did it, or the world's system did it, or maybe your own flesh did it.

When God called Jeremiah as His prophet, Jeremiah was half-scared. He said, "Lord, I don't know if I can do this."

But God answered: "Yes, you can, Son. Stop your knees from knocking. Just be still and listen to Me. Before I ever made Heaven and earth, I knew your name." (Author's paraphrase; see Jeremiah 1:4-8.)

Even if you don't know who your parents are, God knows your name and He has a plan for your life. Nobody ever catches God off guard. He has a divine blueprint for your life.

God says, **"I know the plans I have for you. They're good plans to prosper you and to give you a future and a hope."** (See Jeremiah 29:11.)

Do you believe that?

Change Comes A Little At A Time

You have to plant a vision in your children: a true vision of what God thinks about them and what kind of future He has planned for them. You do it with words that come from the Scriptures, and they come a little at a time.

> Whom shall he teach knowledge? and whom shall he make to understand doctrine? them that are weaned from the milk, and drawn from the breasts.

For precept must be upon precept, precept upon precept;
line upon line, line upon line; here a little, there a little.
                                                    Isaiah 28:9-10

Mom and Dad, you do things a
little at a time. I don't care what
your family situation may be. It's a
circumstance, and maybe even a
bad one, but circumstances can
change – no matter how hopeless
they may look. I don't care if your
children are adults. The situation
can still change.

> **Nobody ever catches
> God off guard. He has
> a divine blueprint
> for your life.**

When Jesus was preaching all those great sermons at the age of 33,
there were probably some mothers sitting around listening and
saying, "Where were You thirty years ago?" I know; I've been in
situations like that.

After hearing the truth preached, don't just say, "That's great! I
wish I'd heard that a long time ago." Instead, say, "Thank God,
I've heard the truth today! Now I know how to pray for my kids."

When praying for your children, ask God to enlighten the eyes of
their understanding. Pray that He will send laborers across their
paths and pray for the Spirit of God to bring conviction to their
hearts. Boldly say, "I command that blindness be removed from
my children's minds, in Jesus' name!"

You have to do righteously concerning your relationship with your
kids. Pray for the Lord to give you wisdom on how to handle them
and talk with them. If you'll do righteously toward them, God will
honor it.

There is no situation that God can't turn around. Not one! If your
family has split apart, He can bring all of you back together again.
If you have a good family, He can make it a great family. Jesus
came to redeem and to restore.

Say What God Says

The world is always lying to you. You'll hear how hopeless everything is. You'll be told stories of how people who are just like you bit the dust and didn't get up. But don't feed on that!

Say what God's Word says: **"A thousand may fall on one side of me and ten thousand on the other side, but it won't come near me! My home may look like it's falling in, but God's Word says no evil shall come nigh my dwelling."** (Author's paraphrase; see Psalm 91:7, 10.)

In Luke 6:46-49, Jesus told about two kinds of houses: those built on the rock and those built on the sand. My house is built on the rock of the Lord Jesus Christ. Does that make me immune from life and its circumstances?

No! God is saying, "The storms of life will beat vehemently against your house, but it won't fall."

The *New American Standard Bible* says:

> Everyone who comes to Me and hears My words and acts on them, I will show you whom he is like:
>
> He is like a man building a house, who dug deep and laid a foundation on the rock; and when a flood occurred, the torrent burst against that house and could not shake it, because it had been well built..
>
> Luke 6:47-48 NASB

God never said the storms wouldn't come.

> When thou passest through the waters, I will be with thee; and through the rivers, they shall not overflow thee: when thou walkest through the fire, thou shalt not be burned; neither shall the flame kindle upon thee.
>
> Isaiah 43:2

We may have tough experiences at times in our lives, but we can walk in victory and keep coming out on the other side like someone who has been raised from the dead.

People will look at us and, with their jaws dropping open, they'll ask, "How did you turn that situation around?"

We can give them the answer. "His name is Jesus! He turned that situation around in my life."

You have to determine you're going to say and do what the redeemed of the Lord says and does. If you feel weak, you have to say to God, "I may look and feel like a dog that was run over and then backed over again, but I say I'm strong in the Lord!"

> **God loves our children more than we will ever be able to love them.**

God will respond, "That's all I want you to say, Son. You do your part and I'll do My part."

When the Israelites reached the Red Sea, Moses may have thought, *Oh boy, we're in trouble now!* But God said, "Hold up that stick, Moses, and I'll part the water" (Exodus 14:16).

When God's people came to the big walls of Jericho, God said to Joshua, "Have the men walk around the city seven times, and I will knock the wall down." They did, and He did! (See Joshua 6.)

Take Authority Over Your Home

If you apply the Word of God to your life, God will perform His Word (Isaiah 55:11). But you need to do it so that God can work on your behalf.

In the midst of your turmoil, He will cry with you, "I know it's bad; I feel bad, too. But if you will speak My Word and believe that I will bring it to pass, I will help you."

Our Heavenly Father saw His Son Jesus being spit upon, beaten to the point of being unrecognizable and nailed to a cross. But now Jesus sits at the right hand of the Father, interceding for your children and mine (Romans 8:34). God loves our children more than we will ever be able to love them.

There is just one important requirement for you to fulfill as a parent: You must be taking authority in your home. You didn't become a parent because you're the most qualified. You aren't head of your home because you have the highest intelligence or the most degrees. You are there by divine appointment. So stand up and take your authority! Don't let the devil put you down.

You might ask, "How can I judge my child for doing something when I do the same things myself?" Luke 6:40 in *The Amplified Bible* says, **"A pupil ... when he is completely trained ... will be like his teacher."** Our children do what we do, not just what we say, so we have to be growing in the grace and knowledge of our Lord Jesus Christ, becoming more like Him every day.

That's our responsibility as parents. We stand in that place of authority, not because we're sinless, but because God put us there. That's why we have to be quick to repent whenever we do wrong.

When we know we've sinned, it only takes a moment to ask forgiveness and to be cleansed.

> If we confess our sins, he is faithful and just to forgive us our sins, and to cleanse us from all unrighteousness.
>
> 1 John 1:9

As the head of my home, I stand washed and cleansed, not because I have lived a perfect life, but because I am forgiven through the blood of Jesus.

My kids know I'm not perfect. I've made mistakes, but I've learned to repent in front of them. It's hard to do sometimes, but I say, "Hon, I'm sorry. That was a stupid thing I said and a dumb thing I did. Will you forgive me?" Then I ask God to forgive me. I'm going to keep growing in God's grace and knowledge.

There is strength in that, not because I have a *perfect past,* but because I have a *perfect God.* It's the grace of God being sufficient in me. His name is Jesus, and you can lean on Him, too.

My Prayer For You And Your Family

I want you to get a picture in your mind of all your loved ones – your spouse, your children, your grandchildren. While you're picturing them, also picture how Jesus prayed in John 17:20. He said: "Father, I pray not only for those who are alive today but for all those yet to be born" (Author's paraphrase).

Jesus prayed three things, and I want to pray them for your family:

> *Heavenly Father, I pray that Mom and Dad will be a tremendous influence over their family.*
>
> *Number one, I pray what Jesus prayed: that you make them one together as members of the Body of Christ, just as You and Jesus are one. May there be unity in this home. May these parents and children walk as close to You as Jesus did. If it weren't possible, Jesus wouldn't have prayed it. So may they continue to grow in Your grace and in Your knowledge.*
>
> *Number two, Father, let the joy of Jesus be manifested in their lives. Let these parents and their kids be known as families of laughter and joy.*
>
> *Number three, Father, Jesus said the world would hate all believers because they are not of this world. He prayed they would not be taken out of this world but be kept from the evil in it. So I pray now, Father, that You keep this family from the evil that's in the world, in Jesus' name. Amen.*

A Prayer You Should Pray For Your Children

There are three things you should pray for your children every day. They are:

1. *Father, I thank You for teaching my children to fear, or reverence, You.*

   Psalm 34:11 says, **"Come, ye children, hearken unto me: I will teach you the fear of the Lord."**

   If your children fear God, it's the beginning of wisdom. With wisdom they will have long life, honor and riches.

2. *Father, surround my kids with a shield of divine favor.*

   Psalm 5:12 says, **"For thou, Lord, wilt bless the righteous; with favour wilt thou compass him as with a shield."**

   This is saying the Lord will surround the righteous with a shield of favor wherever they go. It can cover teachers, the neighborhood kids and their employer. And as an employee, you can pray, *"Father, I thank You that I have divine favor. I pray that people will like me and not even know why."* This is a promise from God.

3. *Father, I ask You to send good friends to my children – godly friends who will sharpen them like iron and cause them to be all You want them to be – and cut away any friends who would drag them down.*

   Proverbs 27:17 says, **"Iron sharpeneth iron; so a man sharpeneth the countenance of his friend."**

You should pray these things in a prayer of thanksgiving every day.

When I get up in the morning, I pray: "Father, I thank You for my children – Sarah, Jessica, Corrie, Tessa, Lauren and John. I believe You're teaching them to fear You. You are surrounding them with a shield of divine favor. You're giving them godly friendships that will sharpen them like iron, making them a mighty man or woman of God. I thank You for doing it in Jesus' name."

God wants to do that for your children. So make this your prayer for them, and then thank Him for it.

CHAPTER 4

Stature = Discipline

And Jesus increased in wisdom and stature, and in favour
with God and man.

Luke 2:52

Let's look at the second part of that verse, which says:

And Jesus increased in ... *stature....*

Jesus matured physically and mentally.

The word we'll use for *stature* is *discipline*.

To grow in stature means Jesus had some discipline, or self-
discipline, about Himself. As He matured, He learned to do what
He was supposed to do when He was supposed to do it. As
Scripture tells us, **He spent much time in prayer.** (See Matthew
14:23, Mark 1:35, Luke 6:12; 9:18, 28; 11:1.)

Children Are Born Undisciplined

The opposite of maturity is immaturity. An immature person has to be watched all the time. He is immature because he has no self-discipline. But a child won't know self-discipline until he has been trained by his parent.

> **There are three things God requires of us: to do justly, to love mercy and to walk humbly.**

Children are born undisciplined. They cry when they want something and when they don't want something, and then they yell in between. That's why they need diapers. They must be trained and disciplined.

As cute and cuddly as little kids can be, if left untrained, they won't be cute and cuddly anymore as they get older. Their behavior turns into rebellion, and then everybody gets upset.

There is a biblical way to handle discipline. We will be very practical in these chapters on the subject of discipline. As mentioned before, God's people aren't like rats in a maze; we are divinely ordered. We have a destination, with a purpose and a plan, not only as the Church but as families and as individuals.

We all have a divine plan and divine call on our lives. But we have to realize that there are some rules to life. It's one thing to get excited about having a vision, but there are rules we have to follow.

That's why a believer can get a ticket for speeding, driving on the road going 57 miles an hour in a 55 mph zone, while an unbeliever goes 90 miles an hour and never gets caught. As the Bible says, **"Judgment must begin at the house of God"** (1 Peter 4:17).

Follow God's Rules

When our family is out in public, I don't discipline other people's children, just my own. I have set a standard for *my* children, not for the children down the street. I want to live according to Micah 6:8, which says:

> He hath shewed thee, O man, what is good; and what doth the Lord require of thee, but to do justly, and to love mercy, and to walk humbly with thy God?

There are three things God requires of His people:

To do justly.

To love mercy.

To walk humbly.

Three Things We Have To Fight

It seems that the number-one statement of all children everywhere is: "But that isn't fair!"

That's why I say to my kids, "That's right, honey; life isn't fair."

The devil is an equal-opportunity hater. He hates everybody the same – a little baby, a middle-aged person or just an old grouch.

Now there are three things we have to fight against on this planet:

1. **The world's system, which is the opposite of whatever God thinks;**
2. **The devil, whom we have authority over in the name of Jesus and by His blood; and**
3. **The flesh, which is the area we are dealing with most of the time, particularly in relationship to people.**

The devil works at attacking the home. As we can see in the Word of God, he hates the home. That's what he attacked right off the bat when he came against Adam and Eve's family in the beginning, and he has been working against the home ever since. The devil caused Adam to be fired from his job, his family to be evicted from their home and their children to be killing each other. But we don't have to be ignorant of the devil's devices.

Provoke Not Your Children

Ephesians 6:4 is a key scripture for the second word of our study, *discipline*.

Often we parents have made our children memorize the first three verses of this chapter from Ephesians, which says:

> Children, obey your parents in the Lord: for this is right.
>
> Honour thy father and mother; which is the first commandment with promise;
>
> That it may be well with thee, and thou mayest live long on the earth.

We make our children memorize these verses, but then we, ourselves, avoid the first part of the fourth verse, which says:

> And, ye fathers, provoke not your children to wrath....

We bypass these words by jumping to the second part, which says:

> ...But bring them up in the nurture and admonition of the Lord.

Now this wording in the *King James Version* is a little flowery, so let me offer a further explanation. The Greek word for *nurture* is *paideia*, which means "child discipline," including directing someone, correcting them and training them in righteousness.

In child training, there must be rules and regulations which lead to either rewards or punishment. You reward your children for keeping the rules, and you punish them when those rules are broken. To nurture is to train by rules and regulations, backed up by rewards and punishments.

Faith Is To Be Passed On To Our Children

When I was in a class on Christian leadership, we were given a test. There were seventeen young men in that class. Our professor said: "Gentlemen, I'm going to give you several pairs of people from the Bible. I want you to pick out which one of the two you consider to be the best leader." He then gave us six pairs. All we had to do was go through our Bible, do some research and choose whom we considered the best leader of the pair.

The first pair given to us was Moses and Joshua. Basically, Moses was a hothead who kept losing his temper. He smote the rock instead of speaking to it, so he wasn't allowed to go into the Promised Land and finish the job he had started. Everybody knows a good leader finishes what he starts, but Moses wasn't able to do that. (See Numbers 20:1-12.)

Joshua was the one who finished the job. He took the Promised Land. He marched around the walls of Jericho until they fell. He got the job done. (See Joshua 1:1-9 and chapter 6.)

So, as great as Moses was, we picked Joshua, seeing him as obviously the better leader of the two.

The second pair given to us was Elijah and Elisha. Elijah had some great miracles and did some great things, but he was constantly griping, murmuring and complaining. He wanted to die, but he wouldn't stand still long enough to let Jezebel kill him. He ran for his life. (See 1 Kings 19.)

Then God said to Elijah, "That's it! I have somebody waiting in the wings to take your place, so you're coming home." God sent down the fiery chariot and Elijah was taken home to be with the Lord. Elisha took his place, asking for a double portion of Elijah's spirit to come on him, and it did. Elisha did twice the miracles that Elijah had done. (See 2 Kings 2.)

So after reading and studying these two prophets, we picked Elisha. There was no doubt to us that Elisha was a better leader than Elijah.

When we had finished our research and made our choices, we turned in the results to the professor. After reading our report, he said, "Gentlemen, you've done a good job of research. Your choices are very factual – but very wrong."

Looking at one another, we said, "But we can't be wrong. There's no way. We went through every scripture."

> **The most important thing we can ever do is pass on the faith to the next generation.**

Then he continued: "Gentlemen, the most important thing on this planet is the work of God. The work of God was going on here before you came; and, if Jesus tarries, the work of God will continue after you are gone.

"When Moses went home to be with the Lord, the work of God continued because he had trained up somebody underneath him named Joshua to continue that work. Yet when Joshua went home to be with the Lord, no successor was left.

"Elijah, though reluctantly, trained up Elisha, because Elisha dogged his heels. He left a successor to continue the work of God, and it flourished. But when Elisha went home to be with the Lord, there was no successor left.

"The most important thing we can ever do is pass on the faith to the next generation: our children."

Then It Goes From *Your* Children To *Theirs*

Parenting is a lifelong, lifetime process. It isn't saying to children, "Well, after your first eighteen years, let's test you out and see how you did." There is no test you can give them after their first 18 years or their first 35 years.

> Children's children are the crown of old men; and the glory
> of children are their fathers.
>
> Proverbs 17:6

We really don't know what kind of parents we've been until we see our grandchildren. If we put enough of the Word of God into our children's hearts that they pass it on to their kids, then we did our job.

In Genesis 18:19 the Lord said of Abraham:

> For I know him, that he will command his children and his household after him *(meaning his grandchildren and all his servants)*, and they shall keep the way of the Lord, to do justice and judgment; that the Lord may bring upon Abraham that which he hath spoken of him. (Author's paraphrase)

In paraphrasing this verse, God was saying: "I will bring these blessings upon Abraham, for I know he won't become a grumpy old man, hoarding all these blessings to himself. He will teach his children how he came across these blessings and he will pass on to them, not only material things, but a knowledge of Me."

The way I see it, my children will inherit my possessions without doing a thing. All I have to do is die; then they will receive all the physical things I have accumulated. But they will never just automatically inherit my knowledge. That has to be earned.

It's my responsibility as a parent to set a table before my children, but they have to eat for themselves. I have to create an atmosphere conducive for them to want and desire it, and then to eat it. I have to make sure I am not provoking my children to wrath by being unreasonable and unjust and in a bad mood all the time.

Set Up Some Rules

How do we keep from provoking our children to wrath?

By setting some rules and regulations for everyone in the house.

For you to have rules and regulations that really work, it's important to remember one point: Don't overdo it. You can't be setting up four hundred rules and regulations. Children won't remember that many. They might remember three – maybe.

As we get further into our study on discipline, I want to remind you (and I will keep reiterating it) that children are children and they do childish things.

If you intend to discipline your kids, make sure you enforce the rules. Don't make a rule if you can't or won't take the time to enforce it.

Don't make idle threats, telling your child, "If you do such-and-such, I'm going to do thus-and-so." Don't make threats unless you mean it, or you'll make a mockery out of the whole system, and your kids won't listen to you. That's when they will start talking back.

If I am not going to take the time to enforce a rule, I don't even want to set that rule.

Train Up A Child

A key verse right here is Proverbs 22:6, which we quoted earlier in our study. Again, it says:

> Train up a child in the way he should go: and when he is old, he will not depart from it.

Notice it says, **Train up a child in** *the way he should go.*

This verse in *The Amplified Bible* reads:

> Train up a child in the way he should go [and in keeping with his individual gift or bent], and when he is old he will not depart from it.

A parent is to train up a child according to his individual bent. That means each child has a gift or bent, a direction in life to be fulfilled.

Be Flexible

Train up a child in the way he should go. The Hebrew word translated *way* in this verse is *derek*. Another place this word appears in the Old Testament is in Proverbs 30:18, 19, which says:

> There be three things which are too wonderful for me, yea, four which I know not:
>
> The way of an eagle in the air; the way of a serpent upon a rock; the way of a ship in the midst of the sea; and the way of a man with a maid.

This passage is dealing with flexibility. We will get into point number four later in our study regarding dating and sex, but for right now let's look at the first three things mentioned in verse 19:

1. **The way of an eagle in the air**

   An eagle will fly out in the morning looking for food. It isn't like a little sparrow or a hummingbird, which is always fluttering and flapping its wings. When a big gust of wind picks up suddenly, the eagle doesn't panic; it simply keeps its wings spread out. Whatever way the wind is blowing, the eagle just rides up over it and comes down on the other side. The eagle is flexible. It may have to turn and make a few adjustments, but it still gets to where it's going.

2. **The way of a serpent upon a rock**

   When I grew up in East Tennessee, I did a lot of trout fishing and spent plenty of time in the mountain streams. During that time, I saw rabbit trails, deer trails and dog trails, but I never saw a snake trail. That's because there is no such thing as a snake trail around those streams.

I've been standing in the middle of many a stream and looked over toward the bank in time to see a copperhead slide out of its nest and into the water. (That's when I left the water!)

I have watched those snakes. They come down across the rocks where the waterfalls are located. If there is a dip in those rocks, they go down on it; if there is a jagged edge, they come up over it.

I never saw one of those snakes get frustrated and say, "Doggone it! There's no rock over here; I have to go down the other way!" That snake never griped about the terrain; it just kept slithering along. Whether faced with a high rock or a puddle of water, it moved right through it, around it or over it. But it always got to where it was going. It was flexible.

3. **The way of a ship in the midst of the sea**

    When a ship leaves England coming to America, the gyroscope is set in the belly of that ship and it knows where it's going. But sometimes there are currents. Sometimes there are twenty- or thirty-foot waves.

    I don't think a sea captain has ever said, "I'm not going over that wave; I'm going right through the middle of it, so that wave had just better get out of my way!"

    A ship will never go through the middle of any wave. It has to ride over it and come down on the other side. It has to be flexible.

    The same is true with parents and how they handle their kids.

If there is a key word in training your children and making rules and regulations for the home, it is *flexible*. You had better be flexible. The moment you get rigid and legalistic is the moment you're going to reap the whirlwind.

I'm not talking against having a standard. I believe in setting high standards; my children will tell you that. But I am also flexible, and here's why: Psalm 127:3 says, **"Lo, children are an heritage of the Lord: and the fruit of the womb is his reward."**

Children are a reward from God to us. They are given to us as a reward. It's our job to train them up and give them back to the Lord so He can use them for His glory.

> **If there is a key word in training your children and making rules for the home, it is *flexible*.**

No Standard

When I was a school administrator, a mom and dad brought their fourteen-year-old son to my office. I had known that family for some time.

When they got into the lobby, I could hear them yelling. Then when they brought the boy into my office, they stood there yelling some more.

Basically, the dad was saying, "This boy is just like his mother, running his mouth all the time. He gives me no respect, and he doesn't hit a lick at nothing!" The mom was saying, "He's just like his dad, sitting around all day watching TV and belching, and he doesn't hit a lick at nothing!"

Pointing at his son, the dad said to me, and I quote: "Mr. McGee, we want you to fix him. We'll back in a little bit." Then they left him there with me.

When the parents had left, I looked at the boy and he looked at me. Obviously we weren't going anywhere with our conversation, so I bought him a soft drink; then we went outside, walked around the parking lot and talked for an hour.

About an hour-and-a-half later, the dad came back. He seemed to be feeling proud of himself for handling the situation, so he said to me, "Well, tell me what happened."

I guess he thought I would just sprinkle some dust like magic, lay my hands on his boy and cast out a few devils – then everything would be wonderful! But I didn't do any of those things. The boy and I just talked.

So the dad said, "Tell me, Joe, why has my son been acting like an idiot?"

I didn't even have to prepare my response. These words just came out: "Dad, your son has been acting like an idiot because he thinks like an idiot. And he thinks like an idiot because he feeds on idiot stuff. Proverbs 23:7 says, 'As a man thinks in his heart, so is he.'"

Children act strange because they think strange. They think strange because they've been feeding on strange ideas. Whatever goes into their eyes and ears is what they'll think about and then do. It's very simple.

Spend Time With Your Kids

Again, as Proverbs 22:6 says, **"Train up a child in the way he should go: and when he is old, he will not depart from it."**

The average dad spends three minutes per day per child in some sort of meaningful conversation. That would be saying something other than comments like, "Sit down and shut up," "Take out the trash," "Clean up your room," "Do your homework," "Feed the dog." Let's say the average mom spends six minutes per day per child. That would come to a grand total of 2.25 twenty-four-hour days out of 365. Perhaps some parents spend more time, some less.

Let's say your child regularly attends church, going three times a week for at least an hour of instruction every time the doors open, and never misses a Sunday or a Wednesday for 52 weeks. If you add up all that time spent in church, it comes to a grand total of approximately 6.5 twenty-four-hour days out of 365.

Since 1852, there has been a compulsory school attendance law in our nation. A child must go to school somewhere – whether public, private or home school – usually for around 180 days out of the year. If you add up all of those days, with six hours a day of uninterrupted instruction, that comes to just over 45 twenty-four-hour days out of 365.

Remember Luke 6:40? Jesus said, **"A pupil is not superior to his teacher, but everyone [when he is] completely trained... will be like his teacher"** (AMP).

A child, when fully taught, will be like his teacher. The child will start to pick up whatever that teacher values. This verse doesn't say the child will know what his teacher knows. That's why a kid can sit in a classroom for nine months and still make an F.

It's been said that the average American child between the ages of eight and eighteen consumes just over seven and a half hours a day of media time (smart phone, computer, television and other devices). Information given out during media time is written on a sixth-grade level and appeals to nothing but the carnal nature.

Now if our kids are consuming 114 days of media time, spending 45 twenty-four-hour days in school and 6 twenty-four hour days in church and 2.25 days communicating with Mom and Dad, is it any wonder that kids act the way they do?

Childproofing The Home

Parents have usually come to me for counseling because they had what they called a "discipline problem."

One mother said, "Mr. McGee, I spanked my toddler five times yesterday." (I don't know if she really did it, but that's what she said.) I could see the frustration in her.

I said, "Mom, that's about four times too many. What's the problem?"

Then she started rattling off: "Well, the kid ate the dog food and the plants. He pulled out all the silverware and got into my pots and pans. Then he took something out of my wallet and flushed it down the toilet; it disappeared just as I got there, and I don't know what it was!"

> **A child, when fully taught, will be just like his teacher (Luke 6:40).**

She wanted to know what she should do with her rebellious toddler.

I said: "Hold it, Mama. You don't have a rebellion problem; you have an ignorance problem. Number one, the dog food should go outside with the dog. Number two, get rid of those real plants and keep plastic plants around the house until your child gets a little older. Number three, go to the hardware store and buy locks to fasten all the drawers. And number four, put your wallet and purse in the top of the closet out of your kid's reach. If you're going to have kids, you need to childproof your home."

A child's playtime is the same as our work time, and children are very diligent workers. When preschoolers and toddlers wake up in the morning, it's as if they are punching a clock. You may think they are just making messes, but they are working. They work all day long at what appears to be destroying property. They can do things like chew the corners off end tables or paint on the walls. They don't have to take lunch breaks or nap breaks; they just work constantly.

When children get through the day, they look back at all they've done and feel so proud of themselves. Then at night they don't have to work at going to sleep; they just pass out. Mom or Dad has to pick up their limp little bodies, put them in bed and cover them up.

I remember reading a story one time about the cruise ship the *Queen Mary* being pulled into dock to be made into a hotel. The smokestacks were to be taken down and reworked. But when a large crane was hooked to the smokestacks to lift them off the deck of the ship, they just exploded into dust. Nothing was left but that swinging crane. Engineers were brought in to find out what had happened, and as it turned out, there were no smokestacks, only about a hundred and twenty coats of epoxy paint. Those smokestacks had just rusted away years ago.

It wouldn't surprise me that, many years from now, maybe during the Millennium, if you went into my house, there wouldn't be any house left; everything would have gone back to the dust.

But no doubt you would be able to see where all of the walls had been. Still standing would be about a hundred and twenty coats of paint! That's because my kids have worked on a continual basis at autographing the walls of our home. That's just the kind of thing children do.

Children Are Like Arrows

As arrows are in the hand of a mighty man; so are children of the youth.

Happy is the man that hath his quiver full of them: they shall not be ashamed, but they shall speak with the enemies in the gate.

Psalm 127:4, 5

People always ask, "How many are in a quiver?" Some say seven; some say twenty-four. I don't know how many there were, but you need to seek God about how many you want in your quiver!

From Psalm 127, let's think about arrows being used in Jewish warfare. How would we find the Israelites back in the Bible going into battle with their quivers full of arrows?

In those days, soldiers didn't buy their arrows at the sporting goods store. Arrows didn't come two dozen in a box with all of them being the same length and the same size; they had to be individually cut from a tree. Can you picture some guy climbing up a tree and cutting off branches to be used in making arrows? That's why no two arrows were ever the same!

Let's imagine what it was like one day when the Israelites were battling against one of their archenemies. An Israeli soldier was standing there, shooting his arrows at the enemy, when all of a sudden he saw this big ugly guy coming at him. The guy was holding one knife in each hand and another between his teeth.

Looking at his enemy, the Israelite said to himself, *He's coming after me! This isn't good!* So he reached into his quiver for an arrow.

But he wasn't looking for just any arrow; he was looking for the biggest, fattest arrow he had ever cut. When he found it, he pulled it from the quiver and set it in his bow. Then he drew it back, aimed it toward that big guy, shot it off and dropped him dead!

When that was done, he thought the battle was over. But then he looked out across the field and saw one fleeing enemy soldier with long, lanky legs. Looking down at his own short legs, he thought, *This will never work. If that guy gets away, he'll tell the other 10,000 enemy soldiers where I am.* He could feel panic rising up inside himself.

Then he thought, *I need another arrow,* so again he reached back in his quiver. But this time he was looking for the longest, skinniest arrow that he had. When he found it, he pulled it out, put it in his bow and shot it away. *Sssssspptt! Boom!* That arrow flew out about 300 yards and dropped the enemy dead. Then the battle was over, and everybody was happy!

All the other soldiers went back to camp for some stew, while he stayed to pick up the spoils of war, but that didn't bother him a bit. As he worked, he sang praises to Jehovah God about how good God was.

As the sun was going down behind the mountain, he had a load of loot packed on his back and was carrying more under his arms and in his pockets. Walking up the path, he saw movement at the top of a rock, and he knew he had a problem: an enemy soldier was hiding behind that rock!

In a flash he dropped all his spoils of war. At the moment it was as if there was no Jehovah God, as if his God had just moved off to some other planet. (That's how it can be sometimes when we are faced with a trial; we can just temporarily forget about God.)

Then panic struck. He thought, *What am I going to do? If I don't get out of here before the sun goes down, I'll be dog meat in the morning!*

So he reached back in his quiver to see if there were any arrows left. Thank God; he had one arrow! Then he pulled it out, but when he saw it, his heart sank to his ankles. It was that good-for-nothing, won't-amount-to-a-hill-of-beans kind of arrow. Every time he had shot one of those arrows, it had hooked away from the target. The only reason he had kept it was because, if necessary, he could use it as a weapon to stab an enemy to death.

Realizing his predicament, he started crying out to God, "God, I'm going to die! Help!"

Then God said, "Put that arrow in the bow."

"But, God, it's no good. It's a bad arrow. It's never going to be good for anything!"

"I told you to put the arrow in the bow!"

"Okay, God, I'll put it in the bow."

Then God said, "Now aim it away from the target, pull it back and let it go."

In obedience he shot it away, and that arrow hooked like a boomerang around the target. *Ssssspptt! Boom!* The enemy behind the rock dropped dead!

Our children are like those arrows. Every arrow is different. Each child will react and respond differently. But they all have a divine purpose. The same basic laws are used for all of them. But as a parent we have to be flexible.

CHAPTER 5

A Child's Respect For Authority

Our children are going to face temptations, tests and trials. That's just a part of life.

The Bible doesn't say they will be immune from such experiences. It does say, however, that **they can go through the water and it won't overtake them, and through the fire and they won't be burned** (Isaiah 43:2). They can come out on the other side and be overcomers.

They will be faced with certain situations that try to lead them off in some other direction, away from God. But with God's Word hidden in their hearts, God can begin dealing with them about it. When they hear a nudge from Him, His Spirit will be speaking to their hearts. But at the same time, the devil will be tempting them through their thoughts or their flesh. (Every day our children are faced with decisions to do both good and bad.) Each time your child needs to make a decision, there is a three-member board meeting going on inside him.

Spirit, Soul, Body

To understand the makeup of every human being, picture a target drawn on a piece of paper with three circles, each one inside the other. Each circle represents a portion of man's nature: spirit, soul and body. The smallest circle in the center is like a bull's eye, and it represents the reborn human spirit. It's surrounded by a larger circle, which represents the soul (the mind, will and emotions). Then that circle is surrounded by an even larger circle, representing the physical body.

In every situation a child's spirit will be saying yes to God while his flesh is saying no to Him. Our born-again, human spirit will side with God, but our flesh will never want to. *Every time* – without exception. The devil will be tempting him by having someone or something try to entice him and lead him away to do wrong. His flesh will respond by saying, "Go ahead and do it!" But his spirit will be saying, "No way! I'm not doing that! Just forget it!" In every situation like this, there will be a tie vote between his flesh and his spirit. That's when his soul will have to break the tie by choosing sides.

> **In every situation a child's spirit will be saying yes to God while his flesh is saying no.**

First Thessalonians 5:23 refers to us as spirit, soul and body:

> And the very God of peace sanctify you wholly; and I pray God your whole spirit and soul and body be preserved blameless unto the coming of our Lord Jesus Christ.

Now I want to give you three scriptures for the words, *spirit, soul* and *body*.

For *spirit*, 2 Corinthians 5:17 says:

> Therefore if any man be in Christ, he is a new creature: old things are passed away; behold, all things are become new.

When we accept Jesus Christ as our Lord and Savior, we are born again – taken from the kingdom of darkness and placed into the kingdom of God. Our human spirit becomes a new creature in Christ.

For *soul*, Romans 12:2 says:

> And be not conformed to this world: but be ye transformed by the *renewing of your mind*, that ye may prove what is that good, and acceptable, and perfect, will of God.

For *body*, Romans 8:23 says:

> ...Even we ourselves groan within ourselves, waiting for the adoption, to wit, the *redemption of our body*.

As an example, let's just say we have a seven-year-old boy named Johnny, who has just been saved by receiving Jesus as the Lord of his life. He has become a new creature in Christ. He knows his name is written in the Lamb's Book of Life, and he is looking forward to Heaven. He has just started reading his Bible and finding out how he should be growing up in the grace and knowledge of his Lord, Jesus Christ.

According to Scripture, Johnny should be busy every day **renewing his mind (his soul) with the Word of God.**

The physical body Johnny lives in here on earth has no good thing in it. At death, it will go back to the dust, so Johnny's flesh will fight against his spirit. If he allowed it to, he would be eating candy until he made himself sick and watching TV until his eyeballs fell out on the carpet. His flesh wants constantly to be sitting on the throne over his inner man – his spirit.

Johnny's spirit will always go with God, but his flesh never will; his spirit will never go with the devil, but his flesh always will. Whether God is leading him or the devil is tempting him, there will always be a tie vote.

Who is left to cast the deciding vote? The soul (Galatians 5:17). That's why God says in Hosea 4:6, **"My people are destroyed for lack of knowledge."**

Our Souls Cast The Deciding Vote

The part that will influence what goes on with every situation we face is not our spirit or our flesh but our soul.

The degree to which our children have the Word of God in them is the degree to which they will make wise decisions in their lives when needed. If they don't know the Word of God, they will be incapable of making wise decisions and their flesh will win out every time. That's why Colossians 3:16 says:

> Let the word of Christ dwell in you richly...

The Spirit of God will bring to our remembrance all of the words Jesus spoke. How do we get the words Jesus spoke into our child's heart? As Isaiah 28:10 says, it will be **"... Precept upon precept; line upon line... here a little, and there a little."** It's giving our child one bite at a time, with lots of repetition.

In Deuteronomy 6:6-7 God said:

> And these words, which I command thee this day, shall be in thine heart:
>
> And thou shalt teach them diligently unto thy children, and shalt talk of them when thou sittest in thine house, and when thou walkest by the way, and when thou liest down, and when thou risest up.

This means we are to be teaching our children the truths of God's Word when we wake up in the morning, when we walk throughout the day, when we sit down and when we lie down. We are to be a constant reminder to them of God's ways and purposes in this life.

In America, parents seem to be trying to train up their children by always giving them *things*. They want their children to have a certain kind of education and to wear a certain kind of clothing. Then after providing their children with all those *things*, the parents wonder why their children don't turn out right.

But their children have never been given God's Word. With no Word, they will have no wisdom. They need wisdom to have a long life and honor and riches here on earth.

As parents it should be our first priority to see that we plant the Word of God in our children's hearts.

Flesh Pulls On Us Like Gravity

One time we were on a trip flying from Abilene, Texas, to Dallas, Texas. That journey was an interesting one, to say the least. When we left Abilene, we were on a small airplane. That little plane had some screws missing from its inner side; it was shaking and rattling, and some black smoke was coming from one of its engines. All of us on board were wondering how far we could get, just hoping and praying we would make it all the way to Dallas.

> **The most important thing we can ever do as parents is to plant the Word of God in our children's hearts.**

After we landed in Dallas and connected with our next flight, we transferred to a much larger airliner. It was like a floating battleship, a massive piece of machinery. It was as if we had gone from Hell to Heaven in one day!

It's hard to imagine how anything as large as that chunk of metal could ever make it off the ground. But there were some physical laws involved. The law of gravity had that plane plastered to the tarmac there at the airport, but when the pilot turned on the engines, the law of thrust came into play, forcing that big chunk of metal to move out from the ramp and onto the runway. Then the power of those engines caused that plane to pick up speed. The law of lift, joining the law of thrust, allowed the plane to leave the runway and overcome the law of gravity.

Now read this carefully: The law of gravity is like our flesh, always wanting to hold us down. The law of thrust is like our spirit, always wanting to get us on the move. According to Romans 8:14, as sons and daughters of God, we are led by the Spirit of God. That means we are going somewhere. We are on the move.

But the pilot could be running that airplane all around the airport. He could be going 200 miles an hour and never involve the law of lift (knowledge of God's Word). He could be moving without ever leaving the ground. The law of thrust and the law of gravity would be canceling each other out all day long.

Many Christians are just like that. They have no real knowledge of God's Word. They have been born again, with their names written in the Lamb's Book of Life. They're staying busy for God, saying: "Praise His holy name! I just hope I can make it to the end, and I hope God helps me sometimes. He ought to be helping me – I'm helping Him."

These believers are running and burning for God, the same way that big airplane was running all around the airport. But is the guy behind the controls ever going to get it off the ground?

To do that, the pilot must have some knowledge. He can pull back that little lever without ever getting off the ground. That's why pilots go to school: to get some knowledge about how to force that big chunk of metal to leave the ground. Once the pilot has the knowledge, he can apply the law of lift with the law of thrust. As a result, the law of gravity will be canceled out and that big airplane will just ease up into the air like a bird.

When that happens, the law of gravity isn't eliminated; it still exists. The moment the law of lift and the law of thrust cease working together, that big piece of metal will drop to the ground like a rock!

The same thing will happen in our lives and in our children's lives if there is no Word at work in us. As the Bible says, sin is crouched at the door and waiting to get us (Genesis 4:7 AMP). Our flesh will alienate us if we give it half a chance. **The Spirit indeed is willing, but the flesh is weak** (Matthew 26:41).

We have to be continually renewing our minds with the Word of God, growing in the knowledge and grace of God.

Again, the degree to which our children know the Word of God is the degree to which they will make wise decisions. When the Word and our spirits are in agreement, the flesh will be canceled out. But it is futile to simply try to get our child's flesh to obey without hiding God's Word in his heart.

That's why our children need to be involved in church, whether it be Sunday school, vacation Bible school, a Bible study or a youth group. They need to get the Word of God into their spirits.

Taking Time To Give A Word To Our Children

As parents, we must get up in the morning and be the number-one cheerleaders for our children by giving them Scripture. I don't mean you need to have a Bible study; it only takes thirty seconds to do this. Speak the Word of God to them, saying something like: "Remember, Honey, you are the head and not the tail; you are above and not beneath. I believe that everything you set your hand to today is going to prosper."

When you do that, your children may just roll their eyes at you. They may be thinking, *There goes Dad – doing that religious thing again.* But you go ahead and do it anyway. The Bible says **God watches over His Word to perform it** (Jeremiah 1:12 AMP). God isn't watching over *your* word to perform it; He's watching over *His* Word.

Your child may say, "Sure, Dad. Right. Big deal. But, you know, I do have this chemistry test today."

Then you can say, "Well, Honey, that's why the Bible says you should study to show yourself approved unto God, a workman that need not be ashamed, but rightly dividing the word of truth" (2 Timothy 2:15).

Ignorance is a terrible thing. The Bible says, "**My people are destroyed for lack of knowledge"** (Hosea 4:6).

As a parent, you must sow that seed in your child. Just remember that when you plant a seed it takes time to grow. When you sow a seed one day, it won't come up that same day; but it *will* come up. Just make sure you keep sowing the Word.

Parents Are Trying To Do Right

After a child is born, the first word he learns is *no*. Where does he learn it? From his parents. About 200 times each day, he hears: "No! Don't do that! Don't touch that!" It seems we spend most of our time either **criticizing, correcting or controlling.**

> It's a sin nature which gives children the inclination to do wrong.

Around the house, parents are always warning their children. Dad says, "Don't put your finger in that outlet – it will bite you!" Mommy says, "Don't touch that iron – it's hot!" There is no problem until the moment those parents turn their backs on that child.

When young parents are walking out of church on Sunday morning, you'll always see little toddlers running around and their moms keep yelling, "Don't run!" Those little kids can be told not to run, but they'll all just keep running. They start right away doing the opposite of what they have been told.

Do you know why kids do the opposite?

It's because those precious little babies were born with a sin nature. It's this sin nature that gives children the inclination to do wrong and to always be saying, "Don't tell me what to do!" The sin nature in all of us says that. It may seem cute when kids are only two years old, but it's rebellion when they get to be twelve.

> The sinful nature wants to do evil, which is just the opposite of what the Spirit wants. And the Spirit gives us desires that are the opposite of what the sinful nature desires. These two forces are constantly fighting each other, so you are not free to carry out your good intentions.
>
> Galatians 5:17 NLT

> When Adam sinned, sin entered the world. Adam's sin brought death, so death spread to everyone, for everyone sinned.
>
> Romans 5:12 NLT

> Therefore if any man be in Christ, he is a new creature: old things are passed away; behold, all things are become new.
>
> 2 Corinthians 5:17

I see this everywhere I go across the country. Moms and dads are trying to do right. They are ever learning but never able to come into the knowledge of the truth.

Maybe your kid is growing up, but as a two-year-old he still has to be restrained sometimes.

One day in the grocery store I saw a mother pushing a cart with her little kid riding in the bottom of it. She was going down the aisle where the ketchup, mayonnaise and pickles were located. Her little boy had his hand stuck out and was pushing jars of pickles off the shelf one at a time. *Boom! Boom! Boom!*

When I came around the corner, there must have been five or six jars already broken. Vinegar was running all over the floor.

I don't know what was holding that mom's attention, but she hadn't even noticed it yet. Then all of a sudden she looked down and saw what had happened. She must have chased that kid all around the store, finally catching him over in the bread section.

Another time we were out shopping. Being summer, it was hot, miserable and sticky. The temperature must have been about 104 degrees. Mothers were out shopping that day, not because it was the leisurely thing to do, but because they had to pick up things that were necessities.

At the check-out counter, I noticed a mother standing there with her child. Her cart was full of merchandise. The child, holding bubble gum in one hand and candy in the other, was pulling on her, saying, "Mama? Mama?" She wasn't responding; she was just standing there, staring off into space.

All of a sudden she turned around, lunged toward the kid and did a belly flop on the cart. Then she jumped up and chased him out into the lobby. Everyone heard it when she caught him. *Slap! Slap! Slap!* When she walked back inside, the child wasn't with her. She came over to the cashier, wrote out a check for the merchandise and walked out.

Many parents are trying to do what's right. They say, "Well, we've heard we need to make our kids obey." That's right; we do. We sometimes have to apply external control over a child's flesh, but first our children must be taught and trained. (See Proverbs 22:6, Isaiah 54:13, Deuteronomy 6:6-9, Psalm 78, Isaiah 28:9-10.)

Setting External Controls

There are two stages of growth that our children go through, which we have to deal with as parents: from newborn to about twelve years of age and from about thirteen years to maturity. Let's consider each of these.

Newborn To Twelve

The time from when they are newborn to about age twelve is what we call the training time. That's when the parent says, "Jump," and the child asks, "How high?"

Our kids must be trained to say, "Yes, Sir," "No, Sir," "Yes, Ma'am," "No, Ma'am." They must be taught, "Do this" and "Don't do that."

As a parent, I am the most powerful influence in my children's lives until they are about twelve. I tell them everything: when to get up, when to go to bed, what to wear, what to eat, where to go, who their friends will be and what they can watch on TV. I am their brain.

This may sound harsh, but it isn't really as severe as it sounds.

Thirteen To Maturity

Thirteen to maturity is when parents have to answer their children's big question, "Why?"

Teens can ask their parents things like, "Mom, why is it important that we believe in the Virgin Birth?" or "Dad, why is it important that we be born again?"

Your children will start asking questions that will make you study. Maybe you don't know why you have been believing certain things. Maybe you just believe that way because your parents believed it. You may say to your child, "That's just the way we believe, so you had better believe that way, too." But that won't work! You have to start teaching your kids about things based on God's Word.

Around the age of thirteen is when children turn into a subculture called teenagers.

It's during this time that what looked and sounded so cute from your child of age two seems more like outright rebellion when he becomes a teenager. He just looks you in the face and says, "I'm not doing that anymore – and you can't make me!"

That's when you'll ask yourself, *What happened?* You thought you had done all you were supposed to do by putting external controls on your child. That worked as long as you were bigger than him and could physically make him behave if he got out of line. But now, all of a sudden, he's as big as you are and can look you eyeball to eyeball. He knows you can't physically control him.

Children Must Be Taught A Little At A Time

The problem is parents miss something very important. So many of them sit in my office, saying, "We did everything the Bible told us to do."

"Exactly what did you do?" I ask.

> **You need to realize that just having your kids in church isn't the automatic answer.**

"Well, we disciplined when we were supposed to and we had our kids in church all the time."

But you need to realize that just having your kids in church isn't the automatic answer.

There are some laws that have to join together. Let's look at Isaiah 28:9-10 again. It says:

> Whom shall he teach knowledge? and whom shall he make to understand doctrine? Them that are weaned from the milk, and drawn from the breasts.

> For precept must be upon precept, precept upon precept; line upon line, line upon line; here a little, and there a little.

If we've been doing things according to this passage and putting the Word of God into our child's heart, by the time he is twelve we will no longer need external controls for the most part, because internal controls have been set within him.

Then the Spirit of God will bring conviction to the Word that has been placed within our children. They won't do a thing just because Mom and Dad said so. They'll do it because God is convicting them and they know it's the right thing to do.

A Parent's Failure

Let's look in the Old Testament at the story of Eli. Eli, who was in full-time ministry, had two sons, Hophni and Phinehas. God was trying to deal with Eli. Speaking to the prophet Samuel, God says:

> In that day I will perform against Eli all things which I have spoken concerning his house: when I begin, I will also make an end.
>
> For I have told him that I will judge his house for ever for the iniquity which he knoweth; because his sons made themselves vile, and he restrained them not.
>
> 1 Samuel 3:12, 13

God was not telling Eli to go talk to his sons, but to restrain them. God was telling him, "Eli, you need to make your sons stop doing what they are doing. They're committing vile acts at the Temple gates, so do something about it."

We know of three times that God had tried to warn the prophet Samuel. After hearing it from God directly, Samuel in turn shared the message with Eli. God was telling Eli to restrain his sons, but Eli wouldn't do it.

Finally, it was as if God said, "That's it. I'm not putting up with it anymore."

Then the Philistines came against Israel.

> And the Philistines fought, and Israel was smitten, and they fled every man into his tent: and there was a very great slaughter; for there fell of Israel thirty thousand footmen.

> And the ark of God was taken; and the two sons of Eli,
> Hophni and Phinehas, were slain.
>
> 1 Samuel 4:10, 11

A runner came and told Eli what had happened; and, as a result, Eli fell backward off his stool, broke his neck and died.

The Prophet's Failure As A Parent

Growing up in Eli's house, Samuel saw all this happen. Then Samuel went on to be the greatest judge and prophet Israel had seen up to that point. On several occasions he interceded on behalf of the nation and God moved mightily through his life.

But do you know what happened when Samuel grew old? It seems that Samuel's own two boys turned out to be worse than Eli's.

> And it came to pass, when Samuel was old, that he made his sons judges over Israel.
>
> And his sons walked not in his ways, but turned aside after lucre, and took bribes, and perverted judgment.
>
> Then all the elders of Israel gathered themselves together, and came to Samuel unto Ramah,
>
> And said unto him, Behold, thou art old, and thy sons walk not in thy ways: now make us a king to judge us like all the nations.
>
> 1 Samuel 8:1, 3-5

The Israelites were saying to Samuel, "You're getting old and are about to die, and we don't want those two bratty, rebellious sons of yours ruling over us. We want a king." But it wasn't the will of God for Israel to have a king.

That's why we as parents can go to church all day long and have miracles happening in our lives and still see our children heading in the wrong direction.

Understand this: The way our children get saved is by being led to the saving knowledge of Jesus. Now it's going to take some prayer over them and the sowing of God's Word into their lives, with our living lives for them to model, but they will be saved. There are several other factors involved.

Now you may be saying, "Well, I love the Lord and I've been going to church all my life, so my children will, too. I just know they're going to grow up to serve Him."

> **Children don't just do what we say; they do what we do.**

But children won't just love God automatically. We have to train them up in the way they should go.

What have you been telling your children about God? Have you been living uprightly before them?

Children don't just do what we say; they do what we do.

Here we see Samuel's reaction to the people's request for a king:

> But the thing displeased Samuel, when they said, Give us a king to judge us. And Samuel prayed unto the Lord.
>
> And the Lord said unto Samuel, Hearken unto the voice of the people in all that they say unto thee: for they have not rejected thee, but they have rejected me, that I should not reign over them.
>
> 1 Samuel 8:6, 7

Samuel tried to talk the people out of having a king by describing to them the demands that would be made as a result. He was saying: "When you have a king to reign over you, you must build him a house. Then he must be provided with chariots, horsemen and soldiers for war. In support of him, you must give your sons and daughters to work for him, as well as a portion of your lands, your seed and your sheep." (Author's paraphrase; see vv. 10-18.)

But the people still had to have their king, and things just went downhill from there. Why? Because a father wouldn't restrain his children and failed to raise his children right. You don't just tell children what to do. Training means showing them over and over and seeing to it that they do it.

No Respect For Authority

The reason I mention this story from God's Word is because today things are not like they were even five years ago. The world is changing. Child abuse is running rampant in our country and children are being beaten every day. Why? Mostly because people don't know how to deal with life, and they get frustrated, angry and upset. This is proof of how much they need the saving grace of the Lord, Jesus Christ.

These days the dark is getting darker while the light is getting brighter. Sin is abounding on this earth, but there is great news: The Bible says, **"Where sin abounded, grace did much more abound"** (Romans 5:20). I don't care how high the devil may stick his head up; God's head will always be higher!

> **There's no authority except what God has established. Those who rebel are resisting God.**

There's an important point having to do with discipline which we must teach our children. They must learn respect for authority. There will be people who misuse them, abuse them and say all manner of evil against them, but our children must be strong in spite of all that.

Maybe the teacher wasn't fair in the way he acted toward your child. But you can't allow your kid to stand up in class and challenge that adult teacher in front of other people. That's wrong. If you let that happen, you will lose before you ever get started.

We parents have to teach our children how to respond to authority. There is a right way to make an appeal.

First Timothy 5:1 talks about **not rebuking an elder harshly but speaking to him (or her) as you would your father (or mother).** It's not wise to let your child stand up in class and call the teacher a knothead.

Matthew 18: 15-17 says you make an appeal by going one on one with someone rather than by confronting him in public. If he won't listen to you, take a witness with you and go to him again. If he still won't listen, then tell it to the church.

There are certain principles our children must learn to follow at home. As I told my children:

"If you don't learn to obey at home, your next step will be refusing to obey at school. By not obeying at school, you will face punishments. First, you may be assigned a lot of written work; then you get grounded from the basketball team, then suspended from school, then expelled. Next, you can get put into juvenile hall, then the county jail, then prison, and eventually the maximum-security prison, perhaps even facing the absolute penalty of death in the electric chair.

"It's progressive, and it gets worse, not better. The sooner you learn to respond to authority, the better your life will be on this planet. You have to know how to respond to authority, because God set up authorities.

"According to Romans 13: 1-3 NIV, **there is no authority except that which God has established, and those who rebel against authority are rebelling against God.** It says rulers are not a terror to those who do right but to those who do wrong. If you do what is right, those in authority will commend you."

Shifting The Blame Or Repenting?

Your kid may be challenging you and your rules, saying, "But it isn't fair!"

That's a shift of guilt. Your child will never repent as long as he can succeed in shifting that guilt in some other direction.

Don't let your child run around saying, "Well, it's so-and-so's fault," or "It's the teacher's fault," or "It's the school's fault." Again, that's a shift of guilt.

By allowing your child to shift the blame, you will never see your child repent. A person will only repent when he truly feels remorse.

Your child may be saying, "I've done something wrong and I have to get it off my chest." The only ways for him to do this would be by shifting the blame to someone or something else or by repenting himself.

As long as he can shift the blame in another direction, he will never repent. Instead, he'll say something like: "It wasn't *my* fault; it was *Billy's* fault. *He's* the one responsible."

If your child doesn't learn to repent, he will never walk in God's favor and have the blessings of God. You have to get to the place where your child can understand this truth. If you don't, he will never know how to repent and he will be living in bondage to sin. The only way any of us can get sin out of our life is by repenting of it and confessing it.

It seems today that self-esteem seminars are being presented everywhere, in churches as well as in the business world. You can find notices for these self-esteem seminars on street corners in every major city in this country. Why? Because people throughout our country are feeling bad about themselves. The devil is doing his job well.

Someone may say, "I'm going to that self-esteem seminar because I feel rotten about myself. The problem must have stemmed from my mother or my father. It has to come from somebody."

I would say to that person, "No, *you're* the problem! Why don't you repent and get that sin out of your life, or forgive them, and let it go? Then you can start living a good life by the power of God's Holy Spirit at work in you."

For the most part, people have never been confronted. Children have grown up in a society being told things like: "It's not your fault; it's your teacher's fault," or "It's your daddy's fault for going off and leaving us," or "It's your mama's fault for doing wrong."

You know, one of the major methods of controlling children in the classroom today is called behavior modification. This involves getting the child to do something you want without letting him know what you're doing. That's called manipulation.

Jesus was a confronter. He didn't mess around when it came to sin. He was not out to condemn the world but to convict people of their sin and to lead them to repentance. It's the devil who *condemns*; it's the Lord Jesus who *convicts*. There is a big difference in these two words.

If we really love our children, we will repent and we will forgive, which means we will turn and go the other way. It's the goodness of God that leads us to repentance (Romans 2:4).

Our children are just looking for someone with authority; they aren't looking for perfect parents. They're saying to themselves, *Will somebody please show me the right way?*

The Goodness Of God

Now that leads me to another Bible story. In Luke's gospel, we find the story of Simon Peter, the fisherman. Peter had been fishing all night long and hadn't caught even one fish. Fish meant money to him, but he hadn't made any money the night before.

The following morning he and his business partners were cleaning their nets on the shore when Jesus stopped by and began speaking to the people. Everybody was crowding in to hear Jesus until He was almost backed into the water, so He asked Peter if He could borrow his boat. Then Jesus stood on the end of the boat and preached to the crowd.

When His sermon was over and the people had gone home, Jesus turned to Peter and said, "Let's go fishing."

Peter's response might have gone something like this:

"Lord, I know You're a good carpenter. I've bought several pieces of Your furniture; my mother even has some of it in her house. We really like it and I recommend it everywhere I go. Now I know You've ministered to a bunch of people today, Lord, and I'm impressed with what you've said and done. But, Lord, let's face it – You don't know anything about fishing.

"I'm the best fisherman there is, and we've been fishing all night long. We went to all the best places, and there aren't any fish out there. The sun is up now, and we can't catch fish in the daytime. That isn't the kind of fishing we do."

But Jesus said to Peter, "I want you to take out your boat and let down your nets for a catch" (Luke 5:4).

So Peter said, "Okay, Lord. For You, we'll go out." I think Peter was just giving the Lord lip service, but he had Jesus sit down in the boat.

Evidently, Peter's buddies didn't go out with them. He probably said, "You guys stay here and finish your work. I'm taking the Lord out fishing."

If you read this account in chapter five of Luke's gospel, you will see that Jesus said to Peter, **"Launch out into the deep, and let down your nets"** (v. 4). Notice He said *nets* – plural. To show you Peter's half-hearted effort, verse 5 says he let down a *net* – singular. So Peter's attitude was all wrong.

But when he dropped the net (singular), things suddenly began to happen. That net filled up and began to break. Then the boat began to sink. Peter forgot all about the Lord. He wasn't consumed with a wonderful, religious *King James* miracle. For him, this meant cash – it was payday!

He started hollering back to shore for help from his partners. "Come quick!" he yelled. "We're losing it!" Then they all brought out their boats. Everybody was throwing out their nets and pulling them back in full of fish.

Peter was probably thinking, *Fish! Cash! I have the market cornered now!*

But on the way back to shore something happened. Peter looked around and saw Jesus there at the end of the boat. The Bible says Peter fell down before Him and said these guilt-ridden words: **"Depart from me; for I am a sinful man, O Lord"** (v. 8).

Do you know what had just hit Peter? An awareness of the goodness of God. He recognized what God had done for him and he was overwhelmed. He didn't feel worthy of what Jesus had done and he couldn't stand it.

It wasn't a lightning bolt from Heaven that struck him because he wouldn't believe God. God didn't have some monster come up and bite off his head. But that's how some people view God.

No Excuse For Child Abuse

I remember some "Christian" films we rented for the children to watch at our vacation Bible school. We had about twenty of them, but after seeing only three, that's all we could take.

One of them was the story of a little kid living in Jamaica. He didn't want to go to Sunday school, so he ran away. He got in a canoe and was paddling toward another island. He planned to hide out there and catch fish every day. *After all,* he thought, *I'm a big boy now and I don't have to go to church if I don't want to.* But then the canoe tipped over, and a big shark came at him. *Chop!* It really mangled him.

The end of the film showed the little boy lying there in bed. His leg was gone, and he was bandaged up, with his arm in a sling. But there in front of him sat a Bible. The film was showing how God did all those bad things to bring the boy back home to Him.

Between that and "an act of God," who would want to go to Heaven? That film even made Hell look kind of good.

Think about it: If God would do that to a little boy, why shouldn't a parent be allowed to beat up on his kid to teach him a thing or two?

Child abuse is illegal, immoral, and just plain wrong. It's a sin.

One man who had served as juvenile judge for thirteen years once said to me: "Joe, in the time I have been on the bench, some of the worst child abusers I have ever seen were born-again Christians who were literally 'beating Hell' out of their kids in the name of the Lord."

But a parent's authority doesn't mean this. Let's look now at the subject of discipline in the home.

CHAPTER 6

Discipline In The Home

Let me start here with this statement of fact: **Discipline without a relationship will breed rebellion in a child.** A parent can't be walking around acting like Atilla the Hun or some five-star general, who barks out a few orders and then disappears. That isn't Biblical parenting.

You can talk to your child until you've turned forty shades of blue, but he won't do what he hears you say; he does what he sees you do.

I have come to realize that the thing I would hate the most in my children is the very thing I found myself guilty of the most.

After watching my children pull some particular stunt, I would ask my wife, "Where did they learn to do that?"

Denise would turn to me in surprise and say, "Go look in the mirror."

"I don't do that," I'd say.

"You're doing it right now," she would reply.

It seems I can get very animated when I talk, so my children get animated when they talk to me – sometimes too much.

Don't Isolate Your Kids

Isolation is the worst punishment a parent could ever give a child.

> **Discipline without relationship will breed rebellion in a child.**

Don't ever get mad at your child and yell out: "Go to your room right now and stay there! You're not getting any supper! You can just stay there the rest of the night!"

When you act like that, I promise you the enemy will be waiting to whisper to him about how unfair and wrong you are. As Proverbs 29:15 says, **"... A child left to himself bringeth his mother to shame."**

God doesn't isolate His children, and you should never isolate yours. What you have to do is confront the situation, deal with it and get past it.

Isolation is the last resort in church discipline (Matthew 18:17).

Kids Should Fear The Rod, Not The Parent

Regarding discipline, if you as parent don't have control in your home, you can forget about everything else. But being in control doesn't mean beating up on your kids.

The child should never fear the parent. He is supposed to fear the rod, so his parents have to teach him that.

Let's look now at the proper use of the rod.

There is a biblical way to use the rod and a biblical time for correction. The parent must learn when and how it is to be used, and how often.

Before anyone gets a wild idea about misusing the rod, let me make a statement right here: Parents' you must never use the rod on your child for doing anything other than that which he has specifically and repeatedly been told not to do.

Don't ever use the rod on your kids because they spilled milk at the table or even knocked out the plate-glass window with a baseball. When was the last time you did something careless?

Remember when making rules and regulations for your household, **it's the goodness of God that leads to repentance, so be flexible.** (See Romans 2:4.)

There are two words in the Bible we need to consider regarding discipline: *chastisement*, which is the use of the rod, and *punishment*, which is discipline for doing something wrong.

Chastisement

Let's look at what the Scriptures say about the use of the rod. There are eighteen verses on this particular subject. I won't give you all eighteen of them, but I highly recommend that you get a concordance and look up all the verses in the book of Proverbs having to do with this subject.

> He that spareth his rod hateth his son: but he that loveth him chasteneth him betimes.
>
> Proverbs 13:24

The word *betimes* comes from the Hebrew word which means "to be up at a task early." If you love your children, you will chasten them early in life to prevent the long-range disaster of an undisciplined life.

Correction is grievous unto him that forsaketh the way: and he that hateth reproof shall die.

Proverbs 15:10

Chasten thy son while there is hope, and let not thy soul spare for his crying.

Proverbs 19:18

Foolishness is bound in the heart of a child; but the rod of correction shall drive it far from him.

Proverbs 22:15

Withhold not correction from the child: for if thou beatest him with the rod, he shall not die. Thou shalt beat him with the rod, and shalt deliver his soul from hell.

Proverbs 23:13, 14

The rod and reproof give wisdom: but a child left to himself bringeth his mother to shame.

Proverbs 29:15

Correct thy son, and he shall give thee rest; yea, he shall give delight unto thy soul.

Proverbs 29:17

Using The Rod

The word *rod* is from a Hebrew word which literally means "stick." Dr. Richard Fugate in his classic book, **What The Bible Says About Child Training** (Tempe, AZ: Altheia, 1980) says, "The word 'rod' is a symbol of God's delegated authority to the human race."

The rod is a neutral object, not like the hand, which is attached to a face. Hands are for protecting and comforting. Slapping with the hand is an insult to which children will react negatively. They identify such use of the hand as personal rejection, while use of the rod is seen as a result of their own rebellion.

Dr. Fugate explains that the rod is a thin wooden stick or a switch that should vary with the size of the child. In other words, a small rod or branch would work on a young child, but a small but firmer rod would be appropriate for an older child.

The purpose behind using the rod is not to beat our children into submission by sheer brute force.

God knew exactly what He was doing when He perfectly planned the universe and our salvation and the use of the rod to break willful rebellion in a child.

State laws vary with regard to disciplining a child. Check with your local library to find out what is allowable in your state. You have to walk in wisdom.

You need to predetermine the reason you would spank, the instrument you would use for spanking and who would be spanked, as well as when, where and how the spanking would take place – all in line with the Word of God and in accordance with the laws of the land. The Bible says, **"... Be ye therefore wise as serpents, and harmless as doves...."** and **"Walk in wisdom toward them that are without..."** (Matthew 10:16; Colossians.4:5).

Let me give you some training about using the rod. There is only one part of our anatomy God made as a place to be struck with the rod of correction. That place is where all our padding is located. This padding isn't just there so we'll be able to sit comfortably.

Think carefully as I repeat a statement I made earlier: You should only discipline your child for being in direct rebellion to what he has specifically and repeatedly been told not to do.

You don't discipline your child for something you didn't explain to him repeatedly and specifically. You should have said plainly, "Don't do this. If you do it, you're going to get a swat for it."

As I said before, you don't spank a child for doing something such as spilling milk. That can, however, involve some discipline. (We will discuss this topic later in the chapter.)

Again, the rod is a switch. (I've heard people refer to this with all kinds of names, like a wooden spoon or bo-bo paddle.)

People have asked, "What's the maximum number of times that I should spank my child on any given day and how many swats should I give him?"

Again, you need to be aware of the laws of the land and remember that the Bible says whatever is not faith is sin (Romans. 14:23). If you can't, with a comfortable and clear conscience, tell someone else how you just disciplined your child, then you're probably doing something wrong. If you have to spank your child more than a couple times a day, the chances are your child is being provoked to wrath and is not just being rebellious (Ephesians 6:4). And if you're striking your child more than two or three times with the rod, chances are you aren't just trying to discipline him but you're angry and are out of control.

You should teach your child to fear the rod, not your hand. Your child should never fear your hand. Remember, your hand is attached to your face via your arm.

I remember one night when I had finished disciplining one of my daughters. After I left her bedroom, she called out, "Daddy, come back!" When I walked back in, she pointed to the rod and said, "Get that out of here." I had left it on the table. I was the guy who had just used that rod on her, yet she called out to me for help. My daughter wasn't afraid of me. I'm not her enemy; I'm her friend. It was the rod she didn't like.

Of course my kids tried to get rid of the rod. They burned it in the fireplace, put it in the trash compactor, gave it to the dog and threw it away. But I just kept getting another one.

I think one of the reasons God tells parents to use the rod is that we have to keep it somewhere in the house and it usually takes some time for us to go get it. That allows us time to think and stay calm.

Too many times children are being struck everywhere on their anatomy except where all their padding is located. I've seen children with welts on them in places where I'm sure the parent wasn't aiming. God wants us to discipline our kids, not to beat them.

> **You should only discipline your child for being in direct rebellion to what he has repeatedly been told not to do.**

So what are you to do?

Get yourself a rod or a little switch. That's Biblical. There is no substitute for using the rod when it's called for.

Be Wise About Punishment

One time I brought home two formal dresses for my older daughters. I had spent a lot of money on them, and the price tags were still attached. I took them upstairs and hung them in the girls' closet.

That evening when we were at the table eating lasagna, I noticed everybody was there except Lauren, our youngest girl, who was five years old at the time.

I asked where she was and was told she was still upstairs, so I called out to her, "Lauren, Honey, come and eat!"

I heard this faint response, "In a minute!"

A few minutes later, I yelled, "Lauren, the food is getting cold!"

"Okay… in a minute!"

When I had finished eating, Lauren still hadn't come downstairs, so I went looking for her. I called out, "Lauren, where are you?"

"I'm in here," she said.

"Where is 'in here'?" I asked.

I walked down the hall looking through all the rooms and finally found her. She was in her older sister's bedroom at the end of the hall, sitting on the closet floor. There was a big grin on her face, and she was holding her plastic safety scissors in her hand.

I must tell you, there's a creative flair about Lauren. She loved scissors, pencils, crayons and Crayola markers. She could be wearing five outfits at one time and have lipstick smeared all around her mouth. She knew grunge before grunge was popular.

Looking down at her, I said, "Honey, what are you doing?"

"I'm working," she said in a sweet little voice.

Then I glanced over and saw those new formals I had hung there earlier. Lauren had been expressing her creative flair by taking her scissors and working on both dresses. She had cut one-inch strips from the hem all the way to the waist and had cut shreds from the wrist to the armpit on the left sleeves. This job had definitely taken both time and diligence with Lauren cutting such straight lines on those dresses. And I could see all the price tags still dangling off the plastic!

I looked down and said, "Honey, we need to go downstairs and eat supper, but we don't need to tell Mommy anything about this right now. Okay?"

While Lauren was eating her lasagna, Denise knew something was wrong because I kept patting Lauren. She asked me, "What are you doing?"

"I'm just eating with my baby," I said. "She didn't get to eat with us, so I'm just going to eat with her."

When we had finished, I said to Denise, "Honey, we have to go upstairs and look at something. Lauren has been really busy." Then I said, "Lauren, tell Mommy what you've done."

"I've been working!" she said. Then Denise got this panicked look on her face. She went upstairs and saw what happened. Now, she didn't go ballistic, but she wasn't too happy!

It seems that, just the week before, Denise had gone to the store to buy some shiny cloth to cut out ribbons for the girls. She had been sitting at the sewing machine cutting strips of that cloth, and Lauren had been watching her every day.

Lauren wasn't meaning to be malicious or destructive; she was just working the way she had seen her mommy work.

There was a time in my life as a father, when, after finding Lauren in that closet, I would have worn out her bottom with my hand. And by doing that, I would have been severely and grossly in sin. But thank God for His Word and for the wisdom of His Word. Scripture calls wisdom **the stability of thy times** (Isaiah 33:6).

I could have given some harsh punishment to my five year old, but instead I spent time repeatedly explaining to Lauren that she didn't ever want to do that again.

And God provided the money for us to buy two more formals.

Punishing Older Kids

Let's say you have older kids. As an example, let's picture the following situation occurring in two different families and being handled in two different ways:

An Angry Dad

Suppose Dad is looking forward to watching a big college football game Saturday afternoon on TV. With a wife and two boys in the house, he works hard to provide for his family. He has worked about sixty hours that week – and now it's Saturday. It has been a long week and he's tired, so he's still upstairs asleep.

When the older boy wakes up, he goes downstairs and starts looking for something to eat. There isn't much left – just a bowl of cereal and a little bit of milk – so he fills a bowl, sits down and starts watching TV, while eating the cereal.

Then Junior wakes up and goes downstairs, holding a blanket in one hand and a teddy bear in the other. He wants something to eat, too, but the cereal box and the milk carton are empty. So he walks over to his big brother and says, "I'm hungry."

But his big brother only replies, "Kid, get out of here!"

"Hey, you got all the cereal!" Junior complains. "I want something to eat, too!"

Unsympathetic, Big Brother merely responds with, "I said for you to get out of here!"

That makes Junior mad, so he lunges at his brother. The bowl of cereal flies into the air and crashes onto the kitchen floor. Then they begin to duke it out. Big Brother wants to punch out Junior's lights, while Junior tries to bite chunks of flesh out of his brother's legs and arms.

Then Mom wakes up and hears all the noise going on downstairs. She rolls over, pokes Dad and says, "Get up! Something's going on downstairs!"

Concerned about what might be happening, Dad jumps out of bed, runs around the foot of the bed and heads down the hall.

The boys can hear their dad moving upstairs, and they know that Atilla the Hun is on his way! Both of them jump off the floor and take off, with Junior running out the back door and Big Brother heading out the front.

As Dad comes around the corner into the kitchen, his feet hit the milk and cereal that are spread across the linoleum floor. *Wham!* Down he goes! Then that sticky mess is attached to his back.

That gets Dad *really* mad! He jumps up and runs out the front door, a stream of foul words pouring from his mouth. So there he is, standing in the front yard on a Saturday morning in only his underwear, with cereal pressed to his back, and he's cussing a blue streak!

Suddenly, he realizes that some of the neighborhood ladies are outside working in their yards, while some of the dads are out doing chores – and they can see him and hear him! So he turns and runs back into the house.

Meeting his wife in the foyer, he yells out, "You raised two idiots!"

Dad stays angry the rest of the day and he misses his favorite ballgame that afternoon.

A Righteous Father

Down the street lives a righteous father who has also been working hard that week. But he hasn't been so busy that he has forsaken the Body of Christ. He still helps by being a blessing to his pastor and his church. By learning the Word of God, he is growing in God's grace and knowledge.

This dad also has two boys. He too is looking forward to the big football game that Saturday, and he too is upstairs asleep.

Big Brother gets up, goes downstairs and mixes the last of the cereal and milk. He turns on the TV in the kitchen to watch the big tractor pull. *Whoommmm! Vrooommm!* He's having a big time.

Then Junior gets up and goes downstairs. He wants some food, too, but his big brother got it all and won't share.

Then Big Brother says, "Get out of here!"

That makes Junior mad, so he lunges at Big Brother and knocks the cereal bowl out of his hand. When it hits the floor, milk runs all over and cereal goes everywhere. Then they start swinging at one another.

When the fighting starts, Mom wakes up, pokes her husband and says, "Hey, wake up!"

Dad gets out of bed, stretches himself and puts on his pants like a civilized man. He calmly walks around the corner of the bed and stops off at the bathroom for a minute. Then he goes downstairs.

As Dad comes down the stairs, the kids don't even hear him. (Isaiah 28:16 says **the righteous don't make haste.**) Then all of a sudden they see him and say, "Oh, no! Dad's up!"

But do they run from him? No! They just stand there, waiting. They know better than to run from Dad. (Proverbs 28:1 says that **the wicked flee when no man pursues but the righteous are as bold as a lion**. A child should be taught never to run from his dad.)

Dad goes straight to the pantry where he keeps the rod hanging on the wall. Then he walks back into the room and says simply, "Okay, what's the problem? What happened?"

Pointing at Junior, Big Brother says, "Look what he did – he broke that cereal bowl!"

Then Junior says, "But I'm hungry, Daddy! He got all the cereal and wouldn't give me any of it!"

Dad says, "Okay, that's enough."

Then he looks at the older boy and says, "Bend over," so the boy bends over the kitchen table. The boy knows this isn't going to feel good because, during the fight, his pajamas got soaked with milk.

Still sleepy, Dad yawns. But holding the rod in his hand, he pulls back his arm and *Swoosh!*

Then Dad turns to the younger brother and says, "Now it's your turn," and he gives the boy one swat on his backside.

Giving the boys a little time to get some feeling back down to their feet, Dad walks to the pantry to hang up the rod. Then he comes back, looks at the older boy and says, "Okay, son, what do you have to say for yourself?"

"I'm sorry, Dad. I should have done what the Bible says: *'Do unto others as you would have others do unto you.'* I should have let my little brother have the rest of my cereal."

"That's right, Son; you should have. Now Junior, what should you have done?"

"I should have done what the Bible says and let my big brother keep that cereal."

"That's right, Son; you should have. Now let's pray together."

When they've knelt down, Dad says to Junior, "Okay, you pray first."

Junior prays, "Father, forgive me for being a jerk and beating up on my big brother. I'm sorry. In Jesus' name. Amen."

Then Dad has his older son pray.

When they're finished, Dad stands up, hugs and kisses both boys and says to them, "Now I want you to clean up this mess before your Mom sees it."

Dad goes back upstairs, walks around the end of the bed, hangs up his pants and gets under the bed covers. Pulling them up around his neck, he looks over at his wife and says, "The ball game comes on at noon. Would you wake

me up at 11:30? I don't want to miss any of the game."
Then he falls off to sleep.

There is a righteous way for a parent to discipline a child, and
there is also a way that will make the parent look like the north
end of a southbound mule. And all of your neighbors will know
which kind of parent you are.

The Past Is Past

> …What doth the Lord require of thee, but to do justly, and to
> love mercy….
>
> Micah 6:8

To do justly requires that you know God's Word and apply it in
your daily living.

To love mercy means for you to be forgiving. If your child repents
for something, you need to forgive him and get on with life.

Unfortunately, parents have memories like elephants. They can
remember everything, and they always want to bring up the past.
They can remind their child of something he had done years
before, saying, "I remember when you did that three years ago. I
remember what you were wearing and who you were with at the
time."

Once you've repented of your sins, the Bible says **your sins have
been removed from you as far as the east is from the west** and
they **will be cast into the depths of the sea** (Psalm 103:12; Micah
7:19). God doesn't remember past sins and He won't keep bringing
them up to you.

So if your child did something in the past, don't keep bringing it
up. The past is past.

Get on with life now and in the future.

Three Rules In Our Home

We had three rules in our home to point out to our kids things they absolutely could not do. These rules could be found displayed throughout the house: on a big piece of poster board, on the bedroom wall, on the refrigerator, on the bathroom mirror, etc.

Rule #1: Don't ever talk back to Mom and Dad.

This is an absolute no-no!

I told my kids: "If you can talk back to me, you'll talk back to your teacher. By talking back to your teacher, you'll be in trouble all the time. Then if you start talking back to your boss, it will get you fired, and I'll have to support you for the rest of your life."

> **If your child did something in the past, don't keep bringing it up. The past is past.**

Rule #2: Don't argue with your brother and sisters.

I told my children: "If you can't get along with your brother and sisters, you won't be able to get along with your fellow students and you'll just stay in trouble. You'll never be able to keep a job because you'll always be fighting with your fellow workers, and I'll be supporting you all your life."

Rule #3: Nobody tells a lie.

Jesus said, "I am the truth," (John 14:6). The Word says that the devil is a liar and the father of all lies (John 8:44). Liars will be found in Hell (Revelation 21:8).

I told my children: "Even the worst sinner you've ever met hates a liar. Nobody – whether sinner or saint – likes a liar. But it seems the easiest thing for a human to do is to tell a lie. So always tell the truth."

Rules And Rewards

In discipline, parents need to do two things for their children:

1. **Set rules for them to follow.**

2. **Have some rewards for their obedience to those rules.**

I have to make sure I am enforcing whatever rules I have made. Sometimes voices get raised. With as many people as there were in our house, words could fly at a rapid pace sometimes. But I knew when they'd reached a certain place and were about to pass the point of no return. That's when I would clap my hands and say, "Time out!" I gave the last words.

Rewards are important. Children need some kind of reward, even if it's just a little sticker on a chart. Then their lives will go a little smoother. So find something as a reward. Just be sure it's something you can afford.

Ask God and believe Him to reward your children. As Scripture says, God is a rewarder. Hebrews 11:6 says, **"... He is a rewarder of them that diligently seek him."** In the book of Revelation, He says, **"To him that overcometh will I give..."** (Revelation 2:7, 17).

You need to have certain rules you'll enforce consistently, but don't have too many rules for your children to follow.

Never Call Your Kid Stupid

Don't yell at your child and call him stupid. He will start thinking, *I must be stupid because my dad said I am.*

While sitting in school one day, suppose he hears the teacher call one of the other kids stupid. Looking at that kid, he thinks, *There's one just like me.* So he goes over and sits down next to him, thinking: *He's stupid and I'm stupid, so we can be stupid together. We'll go to stupid places, do stupid things, listen to stupid music and talk like stupid people, because we are both stupid.*

Death and life are in the power of the tongue: and they that
love it shall eat the fruit thereof.

Proverbs 18:21

Speak Good Words Over Your Kids

It's important that you speak good words over your children. Say,
"I call those things that be not as though they were" (Romans
4:17). Speak words over your kids like those spoken to Gideon and
David: **"You are a mighty man (or woman) of valor, and you will
do great things for God."** (See Judges 6:12, 1 Samuel 26:25.)

Even if your child just bombed out on a test or got caught talking
for the third time in study hall, you have to continue seeing him or
her as God's champion.

There are times when you will have to discipline your child, but
always follow it with the attitude, *Everything's going to be fine. The
sun will come up. God's mercies are new every morning. Life will go on.*

If you'll do that consistently, you won't have to discipline your
kids as much, and they will love you for it. God's peace will be in
your home. But if you don't do what the Word says, you'll be
headed toward child abuse. God doesn't want you to abuse your
kids. He loves your kids and He needs them.

**As we read in Micah 6:8, you are to do justly – but the only way
you can do justly is by putting God's Word inside you.** You need
to be involved in church, listening to your pastor and
fellowshipping together with other believers. You'll realize you're
going through things that someone else has already gone through.
There's nothing new under the sun, so realize God already has the
answers for all your problems.

But remember the statement I made at the beginning of this
chapter: You will never successfully discipline your kids if you
don't have a relationship with them. That can take some time, so
just be patient. Don't try to change everything in one night.

Suggestion For Reading

I want to recommend to you Dr. Richard Fugate's book on the subject of training your kids, which I have quoted in this chapter. It's entitled *What The Bible Says About Child Training.* This is a very good book. It's based on the Word of God and is easy reading, using big print and lots of pictures.

> There's nothing new under the sun. God already has the answers for all your problems.

Many times when I was counseling parents who were having discipline problems, I gave them a copy of this book. I'd tell them to go home, read it and then call me. After reading this book ninety percent of those parents called and said they didn't need to come back in for counseling because they had found their answer.

A Prayer For Repentance

Now maybe you've done the wrong things in raising your kids. I want to give you an opportunity to repent right now. Every parent has done the wrong thing to some extent; we all make mistakes. Many of us have ignorantly tried to parent our kids the way we've seen the world do it.

If you've done that, I just want you to give it to God and ask Him to forgive you of any wrong, of any sin of any abuse you may have committed against your kids. You need to get that feeling of guilt off your back right now. Don't give the devil a place in your life anymore.

Insert your name in the prayer below, and read it believing that God will move mightily on your behalf:

> *Father, there are parents who have done wrong and feel guilty for it, with the devil trying to condemn them. But, Father, right now, I, _____, am coming before You in the name of Jesus to confess my sins. I am admitting now*

that I have done wrong concerning my children, but I am repenting of it and turning from it. I have heard the truth; and not only has the truth set me free, but it will keep me free.

I, _____, will not abuse my children but will love them and train them properly according to Your Word. I am going to do righteously. Therefore, my children will grow up strong and healthy in their bodies and be filled with Your wisdom and Your knowledge in their minds. They will be mighty in their spirits and strengthened by the power of the Holy Spirit in their hearts.

Father, I thank You now for the forgiving power and the cleansing blood of Jesus.

Now that You have forgiven me, Father, I ask that You give me all the practical wisdom I need for successful daily living concerning my children. I look forward a great future with my children, in Jesus' name. Praise God!

CHAPTER 7

Favor With God = Stewardship

And Jesus increased in wisdom and stature, and in favour with God and man.

Luke 2:52

The third part of Luke 2:52 for us to look at is:

And Jesus increased ... *in favour with God....*

This means God was pleased with Him.

The word we'll use for *favor with God* is *stewardship*.

Jesus growing in favor with God means that He was a wise steward over everything He had – His gifts, His talents and His abilities.

A Parable About Stewardship

How do you have favor with God?

In Matthew 25, Jesus told the parable of the talents.

> For the kingdom of heaven is as a man traveling into a far country, who called his own servants, and delivered unto them his goods.
>
> And unto one he gave five talents, to another two, and to another one; to every man according to his several ability; and straightway took his journey.
>
> Then he that had received the five talents went and traded with the same, and made them other five talents.
>
> And likewise he that had received two, he also gained another two.
>
> But he that had received one went and digged in the earth, and hid his lord's money.
>
> After a long time the lord of those servants cometh, and reckoneth with them.
>
> And so he that had received five talents came and brought other five talents, saying, Lord, thou deliveredst unto me five talents: behold, I have gained beside them five talents more.
>
> Matthew 25:14-20

Notice that the King James Version says the talents were given **to every man according to his several ability**. This obviously means that each of them had different abilities.

In this parable Jesus tells about a servant who took five talents and made five more. When the servant reported this to his lord, he was praised. The story continues:

> His lord said unto him, Well done, thou good and faithful servant: thou hast been faithful over a few things, I will make thee ruler over many things: enter thou into the joy of thy Lord.
>
> Matthew 25:21

These same words were spoken to the servant who had two talents and made two more. (See vv. 22, 23.)

But the servant who had one talent didn't use it. He went and buried it. (See vv. 24, 25.) If you don't use it, you lose it.

> His lord answered and said unto him, Thou wicked and slothful servant, thou knewest that I reap where I sowed not, and gather where I have not strawed:
>
> Thou oughtest therefore to have put my money to the exchangers, and then at my coming I should have received mine own with usury.
>
> Take therefore the talent from him, and give it unto him which hath ten talents.
>
> For unto every one that hath shall be given, and he shall have abundance: but from him that hath not shall be taken away even that which he hath.
>
> Matthew 25:26-29

> **God is big on stewardship, so teach your children how to handle their gifts, talents and money.**

What we have here is an illustration of biblical stewardship. We read how two out of three people in this parable had favor with God. I want to please God by being a wise steward over what He has given me.

God is big on stewardship, so **you need to teach your children how to handle their gifts, talents and money.**

You may say, "But we don't have any money."

That means your kids never will never have any if they don't learn how to handle it. Until you are able to steward it, you will never get any. (This subject will be covered in greater detail in a later chapter.)

Teach Your Children About Giving

Every Sunday as we were going into Sunday school, I would stick my hand into my pocket and take out some change for my children to give as their offering.

As I was handing them the coins, I would say, "Here's *your* offering, and *your* offering, and *your* offering." I was so proud to be sending them into church with an offering to give.

One morning after doing this, I went into church and sat down in the pew. As the service was about to start, God began speaking to my spirit. He said, "Son, do you know what you're doing?"

"Yes, Lord, I'm getting ready to have church. I feel really good about it. It's the first Sunday this month that we made it on time."

> There's only one way to have anything on this planet: it's by sowing and reaping.

He said, "But you're teaching your children to give Me pocket change."

"What?"

He said it again: "You are teaching your children to give Me pocket change. When your children are grown and the plate is passed in church, they will drop in a few dollars and feel so good about it. But, Son, if you don't ever get your kids on My financial plan of giving, they may work hard but never really have anything."

There's only one way to have anything on this planet: it's by sowing and reaping.

As the Bible says, **"... With what measure ye mete, it shall be measured to you..."** (Mark 4:24).

Let me give you my own translation of that Scripture verse: "The measuring stick you use to give will be the same measuring stick God uses to give back to you."

If you give a teaspoonful, when God gets ready to give back to you, He will pick up His heavenly teaspoon to use in giving back to you. But it will be good measure, pressed down, shaken together and running over in that teaspoon.

If you give a tablespoonful, He will pick up His heavenly tablespoon, fill it up and give it back to you good measure, pressed down, shaken together and running over.

If you pick up a shovel to use in your giving, He will use a shovel to give back to you.

If you give only pocket change, you will receive pocket change in return.

That's a Bible principle. The measure you use to give is the same measure God uses to give back to you.

Being Faithful Over Little

As Jesus said, **"He that is faithful over little shall be made ruler over much"** (Matthew 25:21). That means the person who isn't faithful over even a little will always wish he had much; but he'll have nothing because he doesn't know how to be faithful over that little bit.

Are you griping because you don't have a new car? Why don't you go home and wash the old one that you have now? Do you want a bigger house? Why don't you go home and fix up the one you live in now?

Being faithful over little will make you ruler over much.

Our society wants everything now. People say, "I want nice... big... new – now!"

People are up to their eyeballs in debt, and if you think things are tough on us today, what do you think life will be like for our children?

Giving And Receiving

The Bible says:

> Praise ye the Lord. Blessed is the man that feareth the Lord, that delighteth greatly in his commandments.
>
> His seed shall be mighty upon earth: the generation of the upright shall be blessed.
>
> Wealth and riches shall be in his house: and his righteousness endureth forever.
>
> Psalm 112:1-3

The New Living Translation reads this way:

> Praise the Lord! How joyful are those who fear the Lord and, delight in obeying his commands.
>
> Their children will be successful everywhere; an entire generation of godly people will be blessed.
>
> They themselves will be wealthy, and their good deeds will last forever.
>
> Psalm 112:1-3 NLT

Here's my summation of Psalm 112:

1. **If we fear God**
2. **And delight in obeying His commands,**
3. **Our children will be successful everywhere.**
4. **They will be blessed.**
5. **They will be wealthy.**
6. **Their good deeds will have eternal value.**

I don't know about you, but that's the kind of life I want my children to have.

God Loves And Blesses A Giver

It is the very nature and character of God to give. He gave His only Son to show His great love for us and He gives us all things richly to enjoy (John 3:16, 1 Timothy 6:17).

Because God is a giver, He loves and blesses those who give. The Bible is full of evidence that demonstrates this fact. I've added my emphasis to just a few verses about giving below:

> **Give and you will receive.** Your gift will return to you in full – pressed down, shaken together to make room for more, running over, and poured into your lap. The amount you give will determine the amount you get back.
>
> Luke 6:38 NLT

> **Give freely and become more wealthy;** be stingy and lose everything. The generous will prosper; those who refresh others will themselves be refreshed.
>
> Proverbs 11:24-25 NLT

> And I have been a constant example of how you can help those in need by working hard. You should remember the words of the Lord Jesus: **"It is more blessed to give than to receive."**
>
> Acts 20:35 NLT

> You must each decide in your heart how much to give. And don't give reluctantly or in response to pressure. "For **God loves a person who gives cheerfully."**
>
> 2 Corinthians 9:7 NLT

Giving Must Become A Habit

Now I don't want to downplay any one of the four topics we're discussing in this book. All four subjects tie together. You can have a vision for your life and you can be really self-disciplined; but if you are always broke, life is just a bummer.

Giving a habit to be developed. There are some people who go through life trying to hold on to everything, but they never have anything. Then there are those who go through life giving it away, and they just don't know what to do with all of it; it just keeps coming back to them (Proverbs 11:24-25).

In the next few chapters we will look at four areas having to do with teaching your child how to have the favor of God:

1. **Self-esteem**

    There are seminars on this subject being held all over the country. This is a legitimate term, and we will be looking at it briefly from the Bible.

2. **Your child's gift from God**

    At the moment of conception every child is gifted by God to do something and succeed at it in this life.

3. **Your child's money**

    Money is something we all need. If you don't have any, life can be tough. But if you don't know how to handle even a little of it, you will never have more. The way more money comes to you is by you being faithful over the little you have now.

4. **Teaching your child about work**

    Every child should learn how to work. Scripture says, **if we don't work, we shouldn't eat.** (2 Thessalonians 3:10). Eating is definitely a good thing to do, and we won't live long without it. Work is part of what God talked to Adam about. He said, "Adam, you're going to have to work by the sweat of your brow if you want to produce anything" (Genesis 3:19). Another verse says, **"The hand of the diligent shall bear rule..."** (Proverbs 12:24).

Let's look now at the subject of self-esteem. This is valuable for every believer. Parents have to learn it first and then teach it to their kids.

CHAPTER 8

The Importance Of Self-Esteem

We need to get a mental picture of the fact that God has placed us on this planet at this time for a specific purpose. It isn't just by accident or happenstance that we were born in this generation and are living and breathing in this very day and hour. We are here by divine appointment. God knows we are here and He wants to use us. He has gifts and talents for each and every member of the Body of Christ.

In Luke 6:46 Jesus asks the question, **"Why do you call Me Lord and don't do what I say?"**

Low self-esteem is nothing more than failing to do what we know is right. The Bible calls self-esteem righteousness! Romans 14:17 reads: **"For the kingdom of God is not meat and drink; but righteousness** (doing what is right), **and peace, and joy in the Holy Ghost"** (Author's paraphrase). We can't do what is right until we know what is right. Once we know the truth (what is right), **the truth will make us free** (John 8:32). As Jesus said, **without Him we can do nothing** (John 15:5).

That's why God gave us the Law in the Old Testament. It was to make it obvious to all of us that we, in ourselves, are out of right relationship with God and to show us the futility of creating some religious system of getting by our own efforts what we can only get by faith in God and His promises.

You know, there is no single factor that has more influence on how successful our children are in school or in the schooling process than what they think about themselves. Proverbs 23:7 says **as someone thinks in his heart, so is he.** We act the way we think, and we think about what we feed on. Self-esteem starts with knowing and then doing the Word of God.

> **Self-esteem starts with knowing and then doing the Word of God.**

We must make sure that the things God has asked us to do are passed on to the next generation.

In Israel today, every teenager – both male and female – serves in the military. Why? Because their country is surrounded by its enemies. Defense is urgent to the Israelis. They don't sit around and debate the issue; it isn't debatable. Their enemies are plotting to kill them night and day, so life is serious for them.

The Israelis have a different mentality. They are concerned with the survival of the next generation. We can read in the Old Testament how God was concerned about future generations; He told parents to get involved with their kids.

Get Involved With Your Next Generation

As parents today, we need to be concerned with the next generation. We need to work at training our kids, praying for them and passing on to them what we know about God's principles, so that they may increase and not diminish. God spoke this to Israel years ago, and He is saying it to His Church today.

In his classic book, *Educational Ideals In The Ancient World* (Grand Rapids, MI: Baker, 1959), William Barclay wrote these words:

> In history no nation has ever set the child in the midst more deliberately than the Jews did. It would not be wrong to say that for the Jew the child was the most important person in the community. The Jew was sure that, of all people, the child was dearest to God. In First Chronicles 16:22, where we read, "Touch not mine anointed, and do my prophets no harm," "touch not mine anointed" referred to school children; and "do my prophets no harm" to their teachers. The Talmud says, "So long as there are children in the schools, Israel's enemies cannot prevail against her." It has to be remembered that Jewish education was entirely religious education. There was no textbook except the Scriptures, and the aim was to train up its disciples in the way of God. The responsibility for educating children was laid fairly and squarely on the parents, and that was true in the days when there were schools, just as much as in the days before schools came into being.
>
> A person cannot inherit their parents' knowledge the same as they might their fortune. The knowledge is there, but each generation has to win it and enter into it for itself. That's why as a parent we must always be able and ready and willing to tell our children the great things that God has done for us.
>
> The education or knowledge to be passed on to the Jewish child was both religious and vocational. Concerning the religious education, on the very first day of school young Jewish boys were awakened before dawn, bathed and dressed in a gown with fringes. The boy's father then took him to the synagogue, and he was put on the reading desk with the roll opened in front of him at Exodus 20:2-26, the passage that tells of God's revelation of the Law to Moses. The passage was read aloud as the passage for the day. He was then taken to the house of his teacher, who showed

him a slate with the alphabet written on it in various combinations with two of the basic texts of the Law. In addition to that, there was one further sentence: "The Law will be my calling." These things the teacher read to the boy, and the boy repeated them after the teacher. The slate was then smeared with honey, and the boy was told to lick it off. This was in memory of Ezekiel's experience when he ate the roll: "And it was in my mouth as honey for sweetness" (Ezekiel 3:1-3). Then the boy was given sweet cakes to eat, with passages from the Law in praise of the Law written on them. You can see how this would leave a lifetime impression on the boy. It was as if to say, this Law, this Word of God, will become your very life, your very existence.

Concerning the vocational education, that father had a duty to teach his son a trade, for the Talmud says: "Whosoever does not teach his son a trade teaches him to steal." The threefold duty of the father was to instruct his son in the Law, to bring him into wedlock and to teach him a handicraft (Proverbs 1:8; 4:1-4; 6:20; 13:1).

If we really believed this, we would be consumed with seeing this message passed on. We would be training up our children to carry on the message of Jesus Christ. It makes no difference what their vocation may be, whether preachers, electricians, plumbers, doctors, lawyers or something else. Our children still must carry the message of Jesus Christ into the next generation while earning a living for themselves and their families.

You Can Receive From God Now

Many of God's people today are just trying to hang on and survive. The world has pumped so much unbelief into us. We're just working at surviving this day, this week, this month, this pay period. But that's not the will of God. We've been listening to a lie.

That's why Romans 12:2 tells us that **every day we have to start renewing our minds.** We have to think the way God thinks. How does He think? *Very* big!

You might be saying, "Well, maybe I need to ask God for something."

According to James 4:2, "**... Ye have not, because ye ask not.**" Jesus said in John 16:24, "**... Ask, and ye shall receive, that your joy may be full.**"

So then you might say, "Okay, I'm going to ask."

But there is a bonus in Heaven. God is saying, "If you ask, I will do above and beyond all you could ask or think."

> Now unto him that is able to do exceeding abundantly above all that we ask or think....
>
> Ephesians 3:20

> For the eyes of the Lord run to and fro throughout the whole earth, to shew Himself strong in the behalf of them whose heart is perfect toward him....
>
> 2 Chronicles 16:9

Are you a candidate for receiving from God?

When you are weak, say, "I am strong." Say: "Lord, here I am." As Jesus said, without Him I can do absolutely, positively, 100 percent nothing. But I have Him today; therefore, **all things are possible to me as one who believes.** (John15:5, Mark 9:23).

This is an attitude. Some people have stolen these principles and converted them into "positive-thinking" seminars. They are making millions of dollars by going around the country preaching on thinking positively, telling people how life would be better if they just changed their attitudes.

This is true. But why don't you **put God's Word in your heart and keep it before your eyes?** (Proverbs 4:20-22) The Word of God is better than a positive attitude. **God watches over His Word to perform it** (Jerermiah 1:12 AMP).

Teaching Stewardship To Your Children

Let me share some statistics that will demonstrate the importance of teaching stewardship to your kids.

Several years ago Moody Bible Institute did a study on the ages that people became born-again believers, confessing Jesus Christ as their Lord and Savior. They determined that 86 percent came to know the Lord before age fifteen; 10 percent between ages fifteen and thirty; but only 4 percent after the age of thirty.

In every evangelistic program I have ever been involved with, we were knocking on doors and trying to reach people over age thirty. We worked hard for that four percent. Never have so many worked so much for so few. We didn't bother with children; we didn't think they could really understand anyway.

> **More than two billion people on the planet today are kids. The field is ready to be harvested!**

One of the churches I attended as a child didn't allow kids to take communion until age twelve. They didn't think children really understood it. So by the time I was twelve, I had just about made up my mind about God. The only reason my friends and I wanted to "get saved" anyhow was so we could take communion; then we would be able to get a "shot glass" and act like we were getting drunk.

As Isaiah 28:9 tells us, we need to start teaching our children the doctrines of God when they are weaned from their mothers. If we wait until they turn twelve before trying to teach them God's Word, the world will have all that time to work on them; and much of a child's character is set by age twelve.

It's not what kids know but how they react to pressure. You show me how a child reacts at age seven, and I will show you how he will react at ages seventeen and forty-seven. People will always react the same. It's a habit, a learned skill. For them to be any different requires a heart change.

Now stewardship is critical here if these statistics are true.

When Jesus taught His disciples about the fields being white unto harvest, He was saying, **"Don't look ahead for the harvest; the harvest is here and now."** (Author's paraphrase; see John 4:35.)

Of the seven billion people on this planet, it's estimated that thirty percent of them are under the age of eighteen. That means more than two billion people on the planet today are kids. The field is ready to be harvested!

Kids Are Born To Believe

Kids are born to believe. When my son was three, if I had told him there was a pink elephant in the backyard, he would have believed me. He would have run to the window, put his nose against the pane and asked, "Where's the pink elephant, Dad?" Then I would have said, "Just kidding, Son." The truth is, I would have been lying.

Children learn about lying and deceit. But they are born to believe, and they are going to believe something. Teach them to believe what God says about them.

Self-Esteem Is A Must

Self-esteem has become a big buzz word in recent years, but it's a legitimate thing. Let's look at a great passage of Scripture from Ephesians 5. There is something hidden here that you might be surprised to see. The Scripture says:

> Therefore as the church is subject unto Christ, so let the wives be to their own husbands in everything.

Husbands, love your wives, even as Christ also loved the church, and gave himself for it;

That he might sanctify and cleanse it with the washing of water by the word,

That he might present it to himself a glorious church, not having spot, or wrinkle, or any such thing; but that it should be holy and without blemish.

So ought men to love their wives as their own bodies. He that loveth his wife loveth himself.

For no man ever yet hated his own flesh; but nourisheth and cherisheth it, even as the Lord the church.

Ephesians 5:24-29

Notice, verse 28 says: **"So ought men to love their wives as their own bodies. He that loveth his wife loveth himself."**

Many times when couples have come to me for counseling, the wife sits there and says, "I wish somebody would teach my husband how to love me more." Whenever I hear that, I just mark it down in my notes: *Wife is here about husband/Husband has possible low self-worth.*

You can't love your spouse any more than you love yourself. If you feel crummy about yourself, that's how you will treat your spouse. You can't treat your spouse any better than you think about yourself. Now this isn't conceit; it's just a fact of human life.

Most of the successful people you will ever meet in this world are people who seem to really know themselves – their good points and their bad points – and they like who they are. They are good folks; they feel comfortable about who they are and good about what they do. They aren't trying to be something they are not.

You can't love your children any more than you love yourself. You have to find out how God sees you and start seeing yourself the same way.

God sees us, not for what we are, but for what we are going to become, because He sees us through the eyes of His Son Jesus Christ, Who paid a high price for us. He sees us redeemed, righteous, justified and sanctified. If He sees us that way, then why should we see ourselves any differently?

Our Enemy, The Devil

You need to remember though that we have an enemy, who is always working against God's people. He goes by the names, *satan* and *the devil*. Our enemy is the liar of all liars. In John 8:44, Jesus described the devil as the father of lies. In Revelation 12:10, he is called the accuser of the brethren.

> **You can't love your children more than you love yourself. Find out how God sees you and see yourself that way.**

It's the devil's mission to come at you and me, at my child and your child, and to always try to tell us how worthless, no-good, stupid, ugly and dumb we are. That's his job, and he's good at it!

Free From Condemnation

But as Scripture says, **"There is therefore now no condemnation to them which are in Christ Jesus..."** (Romans 8:1). We don't have to feel condemned by the devil.

I know what I once was, but I also know what I am now.

> Therefore if any man be in Christ, he is a new creature: old things are passed away; behold, all things are become new.
> 2 Corinthians 5:17

Now that doesn't mean I was made perfect. Even though I am righteous through Christ Jesus, I can stumble and fall on my face seven times a day. But it's my job to get back up, dust myself off, repent and keep moving on.

When I ask God to forgive me, He will.

He removes my sin from me as far as the east is from the west and casts it into the depths of the sea. He sees me free from sin! (Psalm 103:12, Micah 7:19)

If I start bringing up things I've done, He will say, "But I don't remember that."

"Sure you do, Lord. I just did that yesterday. Remember?"

"No, you have repented of it," He says, "and I can't remember it."

God cannot lie (Titus 1:2). If He says He doesn't remember it, He isn't lying to you or kidding you, so don't be reminding Him of it.

He says, "I don't remember your sin; you repented of that, so don't keep bringing it up."

"But I remember it, Lord, and I feel bad about it."

That's the same as saying all that Jesus did wasn't worth anything. If you have repented, then it's done – period. It was buried under His blood. Don't be sticking your hand down into the dirt, grabbing that sin and dragging it back out.

You have to see yourself this way before you can really see your kids that way.

Three Ways To Build Self-Esteem

I am going to give you three simple ways that can be used to build self-esteem or self-worth in your child.

1. **Communicate And Listen – Be Slow To Speak And Quick To Hear (James 1:19).**

Parents are always saying to me, "I've tried to talk to my kids about that, but they won't even listen."

Let me tell you, Mom and Dad, you will never be able to have a deep conversation with your child if you don't first have some seemingly silly conversations with him. If you aren't willing to listen to all the seemingly dumb things your kids have to say, you will never be able to talk to them about the important things. It's called communicating.

I have learned to be a good listener. Sometimes when my children start talking to me, everything sounds so silly. I feel like saying to them: "I'm too busy to listen right now. I have some important things to think about, so you just sit down and be still." But that's no good. I have to be willing to listen to them.

Let me give you a scripture:

> Counsel in the heart of man is like deep water; but a man of understanding will draw it out.
> Proverbs 20:5

I have to look at all six of my kids and know that God has put a gift inside each of them. I don't necessarily know the gifts they have, because I don't have revelation on it. God has to show me the same way He shows them.

I know, however, that, as I listen to my children, **out of the abundance of the heart the mouth will speak** (Matthew 12:34). The desires of each child will be expressed. By listening to them, I will find out what they're interested in. Then I will know what to start praising about them. I want to start promoting my children and what they do, so I make comments like, "You know, you're really good at that, Honey."

I read a story about an artist who tells how God gave him the ability and the talent but that his mom put wings to his gift. When his mom came home one day, she found that her little boy had taken out the ink bottle and had been drawing what he thought were the most beautiful pictures. Of course, he was just scribbling – and he had spilled ink all over everything! Looking back on it, he wondered why his mom didn't give him a good spanking.

But she didn't panic. She walked over and picked up the papers he had been drawing on. Then she said, "Son, I didn't know you could draw so well. That's great!" She must have spent ten minutes just bragging on him. Then she said, "Let's put your pictures up here on the refrigerator to dry, and we'll clean up this mess before your dad gets home."

After that, every time he would draw, his mom just bragged on him. As a result, he became a very famous artist.

A business man told me another story about a time that he had been away on a trip. He said he had really missed his family. But as soon as he walked in the house, he noticed the trash was running over in the kitchen, and it was the job of his fifteen-year-old son to empty the trash. That son came running up to hug his dad's neck, but before the boy could even touch him, Dad unleashed on him, saying, "How come you haven't emptied the trash? I've been gone for five days! Don't you know that it's your job to empty the trash?"

> **If parents don't watch out, they can do little things that can wound their children's spirits.**

The son apologized three times on the way up the stairs, "I'm really sorry, Dad." But his dad just increased his ranting and raving.

When they sat down for supper, Dad's stomach started churning as God began dealing with him, saying: "Your son ran up to hug your neck because he has a relationship with you, and you just killed it over some trash that could have been emptied in about thirty seconds." That businessman realized then that he had to change his ways.

If parents don't watch out, they can do little things every day that can kill their relationships with their children and wound their children's spirits. Parents can still teach and train their children without killing their spirits, but it requires them to be wise stewards.

It's similar to an ant hill. There are some big red ants in Oklahoma. You can kick down an ant hill or stick firecrackers in it and blow it up, but by the next day those ants will build it back up again. However, they will only work at rebuilding that hill for so long; then they give up. I have seen it happen. It looks as if they have packed their suitcases and are moving out, as if to say: "There's no reason to rebuild this hill; somebody just keeps kicking it down. Why should we try again? Why make the effort? It's hopeless."

2. Be Willing To Get Involved With Your Child.

I can't emphasize this enough. Proverbs 27:17 says:

> Iron sharpeneth iron; so a man sharpeneth the countenance of his friend.

This verse is one of the scriptures included in our study on friendship later in this book, but the principle can apply here, as well.

If I am not involved with my children, I have no idea what is going on in their lives. My conversation with them would then become very shallow, with me asking a question like, "How did school go?" I will have no idea if I don't even know what subjects they are taking.

I wonder how many parents do that. The conversation might go something like this:

"How did it go today?" the parent asks.

"Pretty good," the child responds.

The conversation quickly ends with the parent saying simply, "That's good."

Parents like this don't have any idea what their kids are doing, what subjects they're taking, which teachers they have or who their friends are.

Being involved in the basketball games at our school every year, I noticed that about eighty percent of the parents didn't show up for any of the games. To them, basketball time meant "dump and run." It was a time when they could *dump* their kids and then *run* in some other direction. They'd go out to eat, or go to the mall and shop, or go home and spend some time alone. It was like the TV commercial that says, "You pay now – or you pay later." Parents who act like this will pay for it eventually.

I believe we had as close a relationship with some of our high-school kids as they had with their own parents because Denise and I were at so many of their ball games. If I was in town, I would be there. They could depend on me.

Our school was involved in cross-country meets, and my kids were on the team. Sometimes these competitions were in Oklahoma City. It was a two-hour drive to get there, but the race itself took only thirty to forty minutes from start to finish. Besides paying for fees and tolls, it cost me about twenty-seven dollars for McDonald's burgers and fries.

I went to these meets several years in a row, both as a father and as a school administrator, and usually I only saw a few other parents from school. It was the same with basketball games played away from home. The parents would make comments like, "I don't have time to drive all the way over there and back; that would take four hours." Yet several times those same people would come to my office for counseling. They just didn't have enough time for their kids.

Whenever parents don't have time for their kids, it will eventually cost them.

I can talk to my kids about serious things because they know I love them. As Jesus said, **"I know you love Me because you do what I say"** (John 14:23). My kids knew when I was at their ball games or other activities. I knew when they were strong and when they were weak. I went to encourage them, and they knew it.

Even if I was out of town, I would call home and ask my daughter, "How did the game go tonight?"

If she said it didn't go so well, I didn't respond by saying, "Well, Honey, just try harder. You just hang in there now." Instead, I'd say, "Tell me what happened."

Once I got some details, and because I knew her, I could say: "Do you know what your problem is, Honey? You can't dribble looking down at the ball; you have to keep your head up. We're going to get you some training; then you'll know how to do it differently. And after your jump shot, you're too slow coming down the court; you need to pick up some speed." I knew what to say because I knew my kids.

> **Whenever parents don't have time for their kids, it will eventually cost them.**

Denise has said to me many times, **"You know, the most important thing we have done as parents is to have been there for our children."**

Despite numerous mistakes, the best thing we have ever done was to just simply be there for them; if not physically, they knew we were there mentally.

When I talk to my kids, I am a normal parent; but because we have a relationship, I can get specific. As the Scripture says, I am like iron sharpening iron. By being specific I am helping them, and they know that. I am not just flapping my gums and blowing hot air. I know my children. I try to know where their weaknesses are, and I try to point out their strengths, too.

I have said to my kids: "Do you know what your problem is? You're so disorganized. You just don't know what's coming up tomorrow, and you get hit from the backside too many times. So we're going to get you organized. Now it's no big deal. You'll recover from it, and life will go on."

Then I have taken them to the store and bought some of those little organizing books to help bring some order into their lives.

I know where my children are weak and I know how to sharpen them, so they can get better because I spent time with them. When we, as parents, spend time with our kids, that time is never wasted. The same is true with my wife. If I didn't spend time with her, I wouldn't know her either. Even after forty years of marriage, I still need to spend time getting to know her.

Relationship is the key. You really can't practice stewardship until you have established relationship.

3. Help Your Kids To Reflect On Things.

> The most important thing we have done as parents is to have been there for our children.

This is how to make your child feel better about himself. It says in Proverbs 27:19, **"As in water, face reflects face, so the heart of man reflects man"** (Author's paraphrase).

Take some time to sit down and talk with your children. It might only be for five or ten minutes, but it can be well worth it. Even when I was out of town, I would call long distance and try to talk a few minutes with each of the children.

When I first started traveling, the phone bills were eating me alive, so I got an 800 number that cost only a few dollars a month. I could call from anywhere in the United States for only a few cents a minute. This was in the days before cell phones, of course, but I did whatever it took. The phone with that 800 number was in the kitchen; so when I called home, one of the children usually answered, and we talked for a while.

Sometimes I had to remind my children about the things God does for us. That's what God did with Israel. After doing something big, He would say, "Pile up some rocks right here; I want you to remember what I did for you." Then He had them look back at the things He had done for them during certain momentous times.

Sometimes you have to think on the goodness of God. Have a conversation with yourself that goes something like this: *Things aren't looking so good now, but God showed up before, remember? That's right. He did, didn't He?* By doing this, you are encouraging yourself in the Lord.

Sometimes when things got tough and one of my children was going through a trial, I had to make him or her sit down and think for a minute. I'd say: "Look, we've been through things before, and other people have been through them, too. Now let's sit down and think about this. It's just not that big of a deal, so don't let it get you down. God has brought you out before, and He can do it again."

I didn't want my children to lose their joy for life, so I turned into a big cheerleader. You know, the only one God ever kicked when he was down was the devil. Jesus put His foot on the devil's head and took the keys of death and Hell from his hand (Revelation 1:18). When it looks to my children like everything is upside-down and backwards, it's time for me to cheer them on. That's my job.

As parents, we must purpose to be the cheerleaders in our homes. By that, I mean we need to encourage our children with the Word of God. We need to constantly remind them of who God says they are and what God says they can do.

Let's look now at the special gifts we are to use in serving one another as good stewards of God's grace.

CHAPTER 9

Your Child's Gift From God

Everyone is gifted.

> As each one has received a special gift, employ it in serving one another, as good stewards of the manifold grace of God.
> 1 Peter 4:10 NASB

Whether a cook, lawyer, carpenter, electrician, doctor or mechanic, we use our gifts to earn a living by serving our fellow man.

> Having gifts (faculties, talents, qualities) that differ according to the grace given to us, let us use them: [He whose gift is] prophecy, [let him prophesy] according to the proportion of his faith;
>
> [He whose gift is] practical service, let him give himself to serving; he who teaches, to his teaching;
>
> He who exhorts (encourages), to his exhortation; he who contributes, let him do it in simplicity and liberality; he who gives aid and superintends, with zeal and singleness of

mind; he who does acts of mercy, with genuine cheerfulness and joyful eagerness.

Romans 12:6-8 AMP

Speakers And Servers

If anyone speaks, they should do so as one who speaks the very words of God. If anyone serves, they should do so with the strength God provides, so that in all things God may be praised through Jesus Christ. To him be the glory and the power for ever and ever. Amen.

1 Peter 4:11 NIV

At the moment of conception every person was gifted by God to do certain things. Basically, people are divided into two groups: *speakers* or *servers*.

Every person was gifted by God to do certain things.

The world classifies children into two categories: *high achievers* and *thinkers*. These secular terms are used in college testing.

So, every person, whether adult or child, will go into one of these two categories: *speakers* or *servers*.

Speakers are people who like to talk. According to Romans 12, they operate in the gifts of prophecy, teaching, exhorting and administration.

People with the other three gifts – serving, giving and compassion – are the doers; they like to help other people. Kids who have these gifts just can't pass by without helping somebody, and they're the ones always bringing home stray animals. This is a gift of God.

Psalm 139:13-16 in *The Amplified Bible* says this:

For You did form my inward parts; You did knit me together in my mother's womb.

I will confess and praise You for You are fearful and wonderful and for the awful wonder of my birth! Wonderful are Your works, and that my inner self knows right well.

My frame was not hidden from You when I was being formed in secret [and] intricately and curiously wrought [as if embroidered with various colors] in the depths of the earth [a region of darkness and mystery].

Your eyes saw my unformed substance, and in Your book all the days [of my life] were written before ever they took shape, when as yet there was none of them.

Abilities Are From God

These gifts, talents and abilities are from God, but what we do with them is our responsibility.

While attending a school awards banquet, I watched as a student walked across the platform to receive a scholarship to a four-year university which several other students had hoped to win. I commented to the principal the mixed emotions I had about the student winning the scholarship. He replied by telling me what a high grade-point average the student had.

"That may be true," I replied, "but there are several other students just as deserving, if not more so."

I have known both young students and older adults who have gifts which they ride through life but never fully steward. Yet there are others with fewer abilities who give maximum effort. Some children can make an A in a subject without much effort, while others may have to study three hours every night to make that same A. It isn't how many gifts we have but what we do with those gifts that's important to God. **"To whom much is given, much is required"** (Luke 12:48).

We humans judge differently from how God judges, don't we?

But He gives to everyone according to his ability. Each of us has a different ability.

Don't Try To Be Like Somebody Else

Children sometimes get their eyes on somebody else. A young elementary student once said to me, "Mr. McGee, I read my Bible and I pray and I go to church, but I didn't make the baseball team like they did."

I said: "Son, the reason you didn't is because you can't hit the baseball. Some who made the team don't go to church or read their Bible or pray, but they were born with something called eye-hand coordination. You could make the team, but you would need to spend a few hours each week in the batting cage."

Here is what we all need to understand: The Bible says, **"The gifts and calling of God are without repentance"** (Romans 11:29). As mentioned before, these gifts are given by God. You may live your entire life and never serve God with your gift, but He will never take that gift away from you.

A man's gift will make room for him – and money for him, too. That's why some people can make millions of dollars by singing great songs or by investing lots of money on Wall Street and curse God all the way to their graves. Their talents and their abilities are gifts from God. Good stewardship of your gift may prosper you but it will not take you to Heaven.

If we don't explain that to our children, all their lives they will try to be like someone else.

Let's quit frustrating our children by wanting them to be like other children; they can't do it. We have to find out what our children are good at and not push them to be like someone else. My child can go out and practice baseball from now until the sun goes down and never be as good as a professional ball player.

Some have specific gifts from God, such as incredible eye-hand coordination that most people never will have. But others can serve as an inspiration to my children to be the absolute best they can be.

In basketball, whether in college or high school, any point guard who is quick on the court will normally not be a great cross-country runner. There are two kinds of muscles in athletics: a quick-twitch muscle and an elongated muscle.

> **You may live your entire life and never serve God with your gift, but He will never take it away from you.**

The runner with a quick-twitch muscle can win a hundred-yard dash but not do well in a long distance run. He can't last that long because he doesn't have endurance. His muscles are quick, but he can't compete in the long haul.

Another kid who is slow on the court can run five miles and not even be breathing hard. He will beat the others every time because he has a different kind of muscle. That's a gift.

Now as we have read from Romans 12, there are seven different gifts. Every child falls into one of these seven categories and will have a bent toward that gift. But it's important to be sure that our children are seeking the right gift – the one God meant for them to have.

A Dad Trying To Make His Son Follow In His Footsteps

One man whom I knew desired earnestly that his son follow in his footsteps. He was an engineer, and all he wanted was for his son to be an engineer, too. But his son couldn't make it through algebra. I kept telling the dad that his son might never be an engineer, but he was convinced that he would.

You need to realize, Mom and Dad, that gifts don't get passed down. They are not hereditary. I know that's a misconception according to the world, but gifts aren't passed down!

That boy was flunking algebra, and that made him ineligible for basketball. Then he couldn't be with his buddies on the team, so he got really frustrated and started hanging around kids who didn't do anything. He was miserable, and his mom and dad were miserable. But his dad was still determined that his son would be an engineer.

Finally, we had a conference about it. I said: "Dad, your son will never be an engineer. And even if he became one, I would never drive across a bridge or get into an elevator he had built. Math is a major struggle for him. But he really has the gift of speaking. He's quick-witted and runs his mouth continuously, so he would make a great preacher, politician or salesman. He will do something using his mouth, but he will never build any bridges. You need to start finding out how to enhance his gift so that he can do what he's good at."

Now a gift is a tool from God; but if left unchallenged, it will just wither away. You have to steward it, so find out what your child is good at, praise him for it and then start stewarding what he has by taking him places and exposing him to people with a similar gift.

My Two Oldest Daughters And Their Gifts

I will use my two oldest daughters, Sarah and Jessica, as examples of the gifts.

As a school administrator I had an inside track to many of the tests, both secular and Christian, that show the personality gifts our kids were leaning toward. I gave these tests to my children when they were younger. Sarah's main forté was as an administrator while Jessica was an exhorter.

Both girls played on the high-school basketball team. Sarah was involved in student government and Jessica was on the cheerleading squad. They each had a different bent. On the basketball court Sarah and Jessica were the opposite.

Jessica is left-handed, and she was a great little three-point shooter. Her junior year in high school, she won the three-point shooting title at the Oklahoma All-State Festival. She was quick with her hands, which made her great at stealing the basketball.

Now Sarah was not the most talented basketball player on the team. One coach said of her: "This kid is the most intelligent player we have. The problem is, she can't dribble from one end of the court to the other without losing the ball. But she's getting better."

But Sarah was a big contributor to the team, earning respect from the other players. She knew what was going on around her. She was the best of all my kids at passing the ball; then when inside the paint, she was close enough to do her thing and was a good player.

Being administratively-minded, Sarah organized and kept everything put in order, albeit her own version of order. Her notebooks were kept very neat with tabs dividing the subjects. She couldn't do her homework unless things were immaculate in her room. Then once they were, she would go to work.

Before leaving the house, Sarah would stand in front of the mirror for what seemed like hours, getting everything in proper order. She wore makeup and a nice outfit, with a pocketbook to match.

Jessica, on the other hand, could shove a bobby pin in her hair and just throw on a sweat suit before going out the door.

Because Jessica is an exhorter, people like being around her; she has the ability to make everybody laugh and feel good.

Now when it came to money, Sarah knew exactly how much she had in savings and exactly how much to give in church – 10 percent, not 10.1 percent. When we went on vacation, she had saved up her money and knew exactly how much she could spend.

Jessica, on the other hand, wasn't much on saving money, because she is a real giver. Remember the gift of compassion? You could ask her, "How much money do you have?" She would answer, "I don't know; I gave it all away." She wouldn't have any money, but she would have all kinds of things. She would get more things given to her than any child I have ever seen. That's because she is a giver.

Sarah lives life and she loves every minute of it. Her attitude is, "If I have to be somewhere, I might as well be in charge" (administrative bent), whereas Jessica doesn't care who's in charge; she just wants to have a good time (exhortive bent).

Jessica doesn't seem to worry about anything; there is no place in her brain for worry, so things don't clutter her mind. Everybody seems to love her. She just likes being there for people.

The point I am making is this: both Sarah and Jessica have their needs met through two entirely different means; each of them is bent in a different direction. Sarah has gone on to become a college professor, and Jessica got her degree in accounting; both sucessful in their own gifting.

Giftings are different and every child is gifted. Remember, these gifts are without repentance. God will never pull them from anybody; they are His gifts to us.

Don't Use Gifts As An Excuse

While I want my children to know their gifts so that they can begin to steward them and to fulfill God's plan for their lives, I don't want them to use their gifts as a cop-out or an excuse not to do things simply because they aren't good at them. As a matter of fact, the opposite is true.

Years ago, when I was working in management in the electrical manufacturing industry, I attended an in-service workshop one weekend. The instructor gave a talk that has always stayed with me. He said that every individual's job is divided into three parts:

1. **One-third of our job is the part we are very good at and love to do, and we receive many praises when we do it.**

2. **One-third of our job is the part we are qualified to do and will do when required.**

3. **But one-third of every person's job is the part we aren't good at and don't like to do. When we try, we usually receive some criticism, so we avoid it at every opportunity.**

Yet, the success we realize in our jobs, regardless of our vocation, depends on how much time we give to the one-third we are not good at.

> **Giftings are different and every child is gifted.**

So, while we have our children we need to focus on the area in which God has gifted them, there is no excuse for them to avoid those areas of life that aren't as much fun.

Helping Our Kids To Make The Right Choice

As parents, we need to find out what our kids are gifted at and start narrowing down their choices as they go through life.

When we gave a vocational test to our kids, we came up with about twelve careers that each of them would be good at. They each were probably going to follow one of those twelve vocations. Now that was not, 'Thus saith the Lord.' It was just the results of a test, but there was some wisdom attached to it. As the kids got older, they narrowed them down to a handful of possible vocations.

Going into her senior year of high school, Sarah narrowed it down to two areas she might like to pursue. When we were getting ready to go on vacation, she would say, "Hey, Dad, there's a certain kind of school down there. Can we stop in?"

I had a good idea about the direction she would eventually go; I have just always bragged on how good she was. She was so sharp that you wouldn't ever win an argument with her. She would have all the facts nailed down, so she would make a great teacher. Now that's the last thing she thought she would want to be; but unless God led her in some other direction, I would keep feeding the gift until she did one of two things: either consumed it and stewarded it, or choked on it. If she choked on it, she would spit it out and say, "Dad, that's one thing I know I don't want to do!"

Sometimes our kids have to first find out what they *don't* want to do. So many times, because of the way our society is, kids are faced with too many options.

Wasn't it wonderful when we used to go into the ice cream store and have a choice of only three flavors, either chocolate, vanilla or strawberry? Then Baskin-Robbins came along and confused everybody. Long lines developed at the counter as people were trying to decide which of those 31 flavors they wanted. Then along came nearly as many toppings. You almost needed an algebraic equation just to order some ice cream. Then as you walked out the door, the thought would hit you, *You know, I really wanted that other flavor.*

It's as if life has just gotten too complicated. There are too many options. What we parents have to do is to help narrow down those choices in our kids' minds. Then when they get down to it, they will know what to do.

With that in mind, as parents we need to understand our own gifts and callings; then we can be cheerleaders for our kids. They are gifted to do something; and, with God's help, we can help them find out what it is.

There are several good books on this subject that can be found in bookstores. Do some investigating and then test your kids. There are even tests for preschoolers that take only about fifteen minutes. All you have to do is give the test and look at the answers. You will probably say, "That's about what I thought." That's what parents usually find out.

These tests will normally confirm things you already knew. They can help your children in junior high and high school to start narrowing down what they're good at and head them in the right direction. When you find something they like to do, then you can promote it by exposing them to it. This will cost you some time; but, I promise you, it will pay great dividends.

One of the best books to start with would be *Discover Your Children's Gifts* (Grand Rapids, MI: Chosen Books, 1989) by Don and Katie Fortune.

Now let's look into the subject of your child's handling of money.

CHAPTER 10

Your Child's Money

An important principle we must teach our children is how to handle money.

It seems that in this country we have been fed a lie about wealth. For some reason, we've been told that all those rich people got that way by some illegal means. Some people say, "What we should do is take all that money away from the rich people and give it to the poor people; that will make everything right."

If all the money was taken away from the wealthy in this country, in five years most of them would have it back.

As God says in Proverbs 10:4, "**... The hand of the diligent maketh rich.**"

Most wealthy people got that way by working for it. That's how you get wealth, and this can be a real shocker to some people. After watching so much television, they think all rich people are like those scoundrels on TV who got money by doing wrong.

If you think that way, you need to read your Bible. It says those who are hasty to get wealth will lose it. (See Proverbs 28:22.) Either God is a liar or He is telling the truth. (I know which one describes *my* God!)

I like to read about successful people who get things done. A great book I read years ago was, ***Student's Gold,*** which was published by Honor Books in Tulsa, Oklahoma. My favorite chapter was called "The Failure's Hall of Fame," which listed several famous people in history and how many times they failed before succeeding. Diligence was the common thread among them.

One time I was reading a magazine about some of the top businesses in our country. It told about one man's business that services restaurants in airports and provides food on airplanes. But that was only one of about seventeen companies he owned. He once worked as a bellhop in an Oklahoma City hotel. He didn't have a college degree, but he was a successful businessman.

> **If you are without a budget, that means you don't know the "state of your flocks."**

In the article, this businessman gave the top three priorities in his life: number one was God, number two was his family and number three was his job. He supported missionaries and churches and gave away money. This man was a success because he put God first place in his life.

Some people have said, "Rich people are mean, ugly, evil and full of the devil!" Well, if they're really so bad, why is it that everyone is trying so hard to be like them by trying to get more money? Why don't we just quit working, go home, sit down and prop up our feet?

God Wants Us To Succeed

Did you know that the majority of Americans have no budget?

If you are without a budget, that means you don't know the "state of your flocks."

> Be thou diligent to know the state of thy flocks, and look well to thy herds.
>
> Proverbs 27:23

If you don't know the state of your flocks, you can lose what you have.

During counseling sessions, I would often ask, "Do you have a budget?"

The answer so many times was: "No, I don't have any money to budget. But when I get some, then I'll start one."

"If you don't budget now," I'd say, "you won't ever have any money. First you have to find out how much trouble you're in, so you can know what you need to believe God for."

This can be an eye-opener. I remember the first time my wife and I went through this. We were thousands of dollars in debt, and I was depressed – with a capital D! *How did we get here?* A little at a time. Without a budget, we had no idea where our money was going. We might have made a good salary each month, but we were spending every bit of it; we had also fallen into a habit of using credit cards.

This world's system is designed by satan to put us under – to steal, kill and destroy (John 10:10). If we don't realize this, we will be ignorant of the devil's devices and he will take advantage of us.

Kids Must Be Taught About Money

We have to teach our children how to handle their money. Let me give you an example.

I used to always be faced with the chore of going to the grocery store with the wife and children. With a family as big as mine, I was a two-cart shopper. When I showed up, the grocer, who knew me on a first-name basis, would walk with me down the first aisle and we would visit.

Grocery stores are designed in certain ways. It seems that the first area we came to was the bakery, and I would start hearing from my kids: "Daddy, can we have a donut?"

"No, we don't need any donuts today. Keep moving."

By going through a grocery store, I have discovered where Hell can be found on earth: it's the cereal aisle of the store. Have you ever gone down that aisle with children? If so, you know what I mean.

Through the years, I have noticed how that area has expanded. At one time the cereals fit on half of one aisle; now they go all the way down both sides. There is every kind of cereal imaginable. Wheat, rice and oats are all crammed into different shapes and sizes and can be found in various colors.

One of my kids would pick up a box of cereal and say, "Dad, can we buy this one?"

After looking at it, I would say, "Five dollars and eighty-three cents! And we wouldn't get eight bowls of cereal out of that! Put it back on the shelf and get the oatmeal!"

When we had made it all the way through the grocery store, I would go to the check-out stand and write a check for a couple hundred dollars for those two carts filled with groceries. Then all the way home my kids would be crying because they didn't get what they wanted.

Finally, I reached a certain point with the kids, and I got mad the way husbands do sometimes. I told my wife: "I'm never taking the children to the grocery store again – never! You can go by yourself or I'll go by myself, but we will never go as a family again. This just isn't a family function."

But I knew that attitude wasn't from God, so I decided to give the children their own money. Now, that was a real challenge!

Allowances

I had to come up with questions like: *How much do I give them?* and *What are they being paid for?* (Now don't ask me how much allowance you should give your kids; that's between you and your pocketbook.)

Allowances are given to our kids almost gratuitously. But there were times when we had no money for allowances, so we gave our kids little gold stars. In effect we were saying, "That's like an IOU. We'll pay you someday."

Now there are certain chores my kids did at home that they didn't get paid for. If they wore clothes, they laundered them. If they ate off a dish, they washed it. If they used the toilet, they cleaned it. These are just normal household duties.

There's money kids can earn and money they can save. When my kids got their own money, we set up bank accounts in their names.

I remember when they first got their own money. The next time we went to the grocery store, my daughter Corrie said, "Daddy, can I have a donut?"

"Sure, Honey. Did you bring your own money?"

"No, Dad."

"Oh, that's too bad." Then we walked on through the store.

Now that may sound cruel but I was trying to teach her something.

A couple of weeks later we went back to the grocery store, but this time Corrie remembered to take her own money (and she never forgot it again). She said, "Daddy, can I have a donut?"

"Do you have your own money with you?"

"Yes, Sir, I have it right here," and she held out a little red pouch.

"Go ahead, Honey. I'll meet you at the check-out counter."

She came up to me as I was checking out, and I said, "Honey, where's your donut?"

"I don't have it."

"Have you eaten it already?"

"No, Sir."

"Well, where is it?"

"I didn't buy one."

"Why not?"

"Too expensive."

If I had known that would happen, I could have saved thousands of dollars years ago. I found out that kids will spend their parents' money all day long – but not their own! They will squeeze a nickel until it bleeds.

So if you want to save some money, just give your kids their own money. What you give away, you will get back; what you hold on to, you will lose.

Giving

At one time we lived in an area of Missouri where farmers planted thousands of acres of corn. For them to produce a big crop, they had to determine how much seed to put in the ground.

If you want a little crop of corn for the dinner table, just plant two or three rows. But if you plan to sell your crop and use its profit to make house payments, you'd better pull the tractor out of the barn. You can't just take a little pack of seeds, shove them in the ground and say, "We're just believing for a big return, so we need a miracle, God."

As it says in the Bible, "**God gives seed to the sower.**" (See Isaiah 55:10 and 2 Corinthians 9:10.) I tried to teach my children when they were young that they were to be givers.

What we plant, we will reap. If we plant little, we will reap little; if we plant much, we will reap much. Even unbelievers know this. Unfortunately, many Christians don't understand it.

> **What we plant, we will reap. If we plant little, we will reap little; if we plant much, we will reap much.**

The inclination of our sin nature is to hold on to things, always using words like *me, I, my, want, keep* and *hoard*. With an attitude like this, we would never have a thing. The only way we can beat this world's system and the devil is by getting on God's financial plan, which is a plan of giving. Once we hit that path, there is nothing that can stop God from giving back to us.

We are responsible to plant this truth into our children. If we don't, when they grow up, they'll stay in debt all their lives. They will be struggling to always make ends meet. They'll be using an old, broken frying pan and driving a beat-up old car. They will never have anything without a knowledge of the truth. They have to go to work – which is a part of it – but they also have to start giving. These two principles of working and giving have to be used together.

Remember in Psalm 112:1-3 we are told that **parents who fear the Lord and delight greatly in His commandments will see their children grow up to be mighty on this planet. Wealth and riches will be in their house and their righteousness (or right doing) will endure forever.**

The earlier we start teaching these principles to our kids the better. God will honor the faith of a child.

I have seen one of my daughters, in particular, get things, and it just blows me away. Why does this happen to her? Because she is a giver. I have watched her. She doesn't think a thing about it; she just gives with a pure heart and loves doing it. Seeing that, I think, *Dear Lord, give me convictions like that.*

> Be not deceived; God is not mocked: for whatsoever a man soweth, that shall he also reap.
>
> Galatians 6:7

This is God's law, and it's a law that we must put into our children. If they are to carry on the work of God, they can't do it if they are completely broke. They must get their needs met and then have enough left over to give to others.

The Bible says, **"Feed the flock of God…"** (1 Peter 5:2). We can't be of help to the flock of God when we're broke. First, our needs have to be met; then we will be able to help feed the flock of God.

Savings

Now regarding money, savings is a big thing in our family. Proverbs 3:10 says, **"So shall thy barns be filled with plenty…."** Your "barn" is like your savings account. When they were younger, I told my kids if they didn't spend all of the money given to them in their allowance, I would take whatever amount they had left at the end of the month and match it dollar for dollar in a savings account.

My kids were allowed to get into their savings accounts only twice a year: when we went on vacation in the summer and at Christmas time. At these times, they could take out all but $100. That $100 stayed in, because that's the original amount I used to open their accounts.

Sometimes my kids would say something like: "Hey, Dad, I saw this *great* sale! It's 75 percent off! Just let me take some from my savings account. I promise that I'll put it right back in!"

"No way! Forget it," I'd say.

When I was younger I used to spend every penny that I had. If something was on sale, I bought it. That's how I got so deeply into debt. I always got what I wanted; but then when it wore out, I was still paying for it. It's a sick feeling to still be paying for something that's already been thrown in the trash can.

I didn't feel too smart about what I had done, and I don't want my kids to ever have to go through that. Of course, there are things our kids will have to learn on their own, but there are principles we can put to work in them ahead of time. You have to determine what's right for your family in this area, but you need a plan.

Let's look now into the topic of teaching your children about work.

CHAPTER 11

Teaching Your Child About Work

There are two words in the Bible every parent should be familiar with: *work* and *diligence*. (I've emphasized them below.)

Work

> He also that is slothful in his **work** is brother to him that is a great waster.
>
> Proverbs 18:9

> For even when we were with you, this we commanded you, that if any would not **work**, neither should he eat.

> For we hear that there are some which walk among you disorderly, **working** not at all, but are busybodies.

> Now them that are such we command and exhort by our Lord Jesus Christ, that with quietness they **work**, and eat their own bread.
>
> 2 Thessalonians 3:10-12

Diligence

He becometh poor that dealeth with a slack hand: but the hand of the **diligent** maketh rich.

Proverbs 10:4

The hand of the **diligent** shall bear rule: but the slothful shall be under tribute.

Proverbs 12:24

The slothful man roasteth not that which he took in hunting: but the substance of a **diligent** man is precious.

Proverbs 12:27

The soul of the sluggard desireth, and hath nothing: but the soul of the **diligent** shall be made fat.

Proverbs 13:4

The thoughts of the **diligent** tend only to plenteousness; but of every one that is hasty only to want.

Proverbs 21:5

Seest thou a man **diligent** in his business? he shall stand before kings; he shall not stand before mean men.

Proverbs 22:29

Work is part of God's plan for our lives, and there are great rewards for those who are diligent in their work. Good work habits begin in the home.

Jobs My Kids Do At Home

Let me tell you, there were lots of jobs my kids were involved in around our house. For instance, I remember when my son was only four years old he could make his own bed. He didn't do a very good job of it, but he still did it and was thrilled to do it. I encouraged him every chance I got. Of course, it didn't stay that way long; in an hour his whole bedroom could be torn to pieces and look like a tornado had gone through twice – going through once, then backing up and going through again!

So don't get any images of life around our house being perfect. There were days when everything looked wonderful and other days when it looked like a riot hit the night before. It was up to me, the parent, to set some standards for my children.

> **Work is part of God's plan for our lives. There are great rewards for those who are diligent in their work.**

It's important to set a standard for chore participation in your home. When my kids were growing up, Denise and I required thirty minutes of work from each child per day and a couple of hours on the weekends.

It can vary depending on your situation, but take time to create a plan. Think through what needs to be done around the house and take into account the age and skill level of your kids. Understand that they are going to need to be trained to work the same way they are trained in the Word. This will take time. Consistency is important, but don't be afraid to change something if you see that a change is needed. Be flexible.

Kids like to help. It makes them feel that they are a part of the family. I'm not saying your children are going to be excited to do their chores every day, but by giving them responsibilities you create the feeling of a team in your home. The best way to foster this is through age-appropriate jobs.

According to research, children with regular chores have higher self-esteem. They tend to be more responsible. They're better able to deal with frustrations, and they have a better understanding of the benefits of delayed gratification.

This process will take training. At times you may feel as if it would just be easier to make the bed and take out the trash yourself. At least it would be done more quickly. But that isn't going to help your children. Be patient with them. They may not do it as well as you do, but that's how they learn. Train, but don't be overly critical or make fun of their work. Understand that the quality of their work will improve over time.

Our Home Is A Blessing

Usually, Friday night was family night at our house. I normally fly out on Saturday mornings to hold seminars, so we didn't do any chores on Friday nights; we did "family things."

Home was a fun place for us. Our freezer was full of food, and we had lots of things to play with around the house, like basketball goals, volleyball nets, video games, bikes. You name it – we had it. We had a swimming pool in the backyard and a concrete area to play basketball in the front yard.

Our house was located out in the country on two-and-a-half acres at the back of a mountain. It was a great place to live!

At one time we lived in an older small house, measuring 900 square feet, with carpet that had big chunks out of it. It was all we could afford at the time, but I was believing God for something better. Success doesn't come overnight; it comes with time. It won't just be dumped on you or brought down the chimney by Santa Claus; it comes by working, by believing God and by setting your goals.

Our home in the country wasn't just dropped out of an airplane. It took years of saving and planning. But it was what we wanted. Some people might think it was a strange place to live, but we loved it. And it was our home! But it didn't just happen. We didn't receive a check in the mail to pay for it.

Our children saw us put the principles of working and trusting God into operation.

In Proverbs 16:3, we read: **"Commit thy works unto the Lord, and thy thoughts shall be established."** Verse 9 says, **"A man's heart deviseth his way: but the Lord directeth his steps."**

A principle in the Word of God tells us that when we do something, God does something. We walk around the walls, and God knocks them down. We lift up the staff, and He parts the waters. We make the mud, and He opens the eyes.

As we see in Proverbs 16:3 and 9, there are four steps in this process:

> **Verse 3:**
>
> 1. **We commit our works (prayers)** – *Something we do.*
>
> 2. **God establishes our thoughts** – *Something God does.*
>
> **Verse 9:**
>
> 3. **Man devises his way (makes plans)** – *Something we do.*
>
> 4. **God orders his steps** – *Something God does.*

If I pray about a situation, God will give me thoughts to think. With those thoughts, I write down my plans. As I walk out those plans, the Lord orders my steps.

> **I'm helping my children reach God's best for them by teaching them good work habits at home.**

For us to accomplish God's plans for our lives will take work. I'm helping my children reach God's best for them by teaching them good work habits at home.

> "For I know the plans I have for you," declares the Lord, "plans to prosper you and not to harm you, plans to give you hope and a future."
>
> Jeremiah 29:11 NIV

God plans for us to prosper. We flow with Him by working and being diligent.

These days it seems children are always saying, "I want it – and I want it now!" The Bible teaches us that man should work and work diligently. The basic law of sowing and reaping taught throughout the Bible is involved here. In order to harvest, we must plant. So we need to teach our kids how to work while they are still at home and how to enjoy the fruits of their labor.

That's why when many children grow up and get married, they can't even boil water. They were never allowed in the kitchen because their parents didn't want them to make a mess. But they can't learn if they aren't taught, even though they might make a mess until they do learn.

> Sometimes we have to stand around and tell our kids what to do, step by step, one thing at a time.

When you have kids in the house, there's probably going to be a mess somewhere. We seemed to be constantly patching up something around our place. We even had to replace a few doors because of big holes which just suddenly appeared. It's amazing what kids can break, tear up and wear out.

Adjustments Must Be Made

Sometimes we had to go four or five days without doing any work around our house. Sports seasons were some of those times.

When it was time to eat, we had to first wash a dish. When we needed something to wear, we had to go through all the piles of clothes and pick out something.

Sometimes when I teach people these principles of parenting, they think my house must be an immaculate place in which to live. But that just isn't true. With all the kids around our house, it's just a regular place.

But what we have – and what you need to have – is a standard. Our children knew when we got five days behind on chores. They knew when Saturday came, they owed me two hours of manual labor and they knew there was plenty of work to do. So it was an all-out effort and they'd work together.

Sometimes we have to stand around and tell our kids what to do, step by step, one thing at a time. I say, "Now I want you to pick this up and carry it right over there." But everything gets done.

Keep A Schedule

When it comes to chores, you need to have a list. Make a job description for each child, showing a list of things he or she is to do, and stick it on the refrigerator. Then put a check mark by each job as it gets done.

But remember this: even if your child did a great job yesterday, the natural tendency is for him to be lazy tomorrow. He will just want to eat and sleep. That's the sin nature. He will never want to do anything if he doesn't have a goal to reach for.

So you may want to get a calendar that your kid can use for keeping a schedule. I tried to keep an updated social calendar for all my children, so I knew where they were even before they did. It may sound a little complicated, but it seemed to work well.

There are things you can do to help your child get his life planned out and give it some structure. Life isn't perfect; it can be pure chaos at times. All kinds of things which you don't have scheduled can happen, but without a plan, you won't know how to recover. You may get hit with a tidal wave, but you can't just lie there and rest; you have to get up and start moving. You have to recoup and get back to doing what you had planned to do.

When Under Pressure

As an example, Denise and I were getting ready to leave to hold a marriage seminar in San Antonio, Texas. I had just come home from St. Louis, where I had held three meetings back to back. When I came home, my favorite white shirts needed to be laundered, but I had forgotten. I had even written a reminder in my calendar: "Put shirts in laundry." But I didn't read it.

On the morning we were to leave town, we woke up at five o'clock and were busy getting ready to go when, all of a sudden, I remembered those shirts. I quickly threw them in the washing machine. Then after changing them to the dryer, I plugged in two irons. Denise was going to iron some of them while Sarah ironed the others.

Then while I was packing up boxes for the trip, I suddenly heard Denise's voice, and the sound I heard wasn't good. It seems one of the girls had borrowed a dark, navy-blue headband, and it had been thrown in the washer with my white shirts. As a result, my favorite white shirts had taken on an acid-rain look.

We had to be at the airport in 35 minutes. What was I to do?

Sarah said, "Dad, you're going to be late."

My response to her was simply: "Just go out and get in the car!"

As we were driving to the airport, Denise said, "What are we going to do?"

"I don't know," I said. "Let's just drive and I'll think a minute." I thought, *What am I going to do about shirts? I can't show up in those hippie-looking shirts.*

Then as we were driving by the shopping mall, I suddenly said, "There's a clothing store! I'll just go in and buy some new shirts." So we stopped and I ran inside. I said to the salesman, "I need some shirts!" Then I grabbed up the shirts and wrote out a check.

By the time we had made it to the airport, not only had we missed our plane, but I had gotten a speeding ticket on the way.

Standing there, Sarah was watching me under pressure. She said, "Daddy, you missed your plane. What are you going to do?"

"Well, Honey, there are lots of airplanes. Another one will be flying out sometime. We'll just find one going somewhere, and we'll get there."

And we did. It was just thirty minutes before the meeting started when we landed, and I had to change clothes in the airport, but we made it on time to the meeting.

Things rarely go as planned. Be aware that your children are watching you in good times and in bad.

In Matthew 5:9, we read, **"Blessed are the peacemakers."** A peacemaker is a problem solver. Every day we will be faced with problems and inconveniences. We need to set an example for our children by staying cool under pressure. We are blessed and we've been created to be problem solvers. Jesus couldn't go from point A to point B without someone needing something from Him or having a storm pop up nearby, but He met each situation with a solution. In Him we can be face the day's events and be problem solvers, too.

Don't Waste Money

Sometimes when I'm trying to teach my kids about work, I get onto them about wasting money. Do you ever do that? It really upsets me. I am always reminding them, "Don't waste money!" Speaking of some particular situation, I will say, "Do you know how much money that cost us?" Then I go into a long dissertation.

That's why the Bible says those three things in Micah 6:8, which we read earlier in our study. Again, that verse says:

> ...What doth the Lord require of thee, but to do justly, and to love mercy, and to walk humbly with thy God?

Sometimes the very thing you get on to your kids about is the very thing you make the mistake of doing yourself.

Let me give you an example of how we can react to certain situations.

I remember when I had really been getting on to my kids about money. I had just finished working on the annual family budget and was becoming like a broken record. I kept saying, "Do you know how much money that cost us?" I would be nice sometimes and we would laugh, but other times I would get really tough with them.

The previous fall I had bought two bales of hay to spread on the ground so that the grass would grow between all the huge rocks that lay around our property. One of those bales had been left sitting out all winter until green grass was starting to grow out the top of it.

Denise reminded me of it, saying, "Are you going to do something with that bale of hay on the back hill behind the house? I'd appreciate it if you would get it out of the backyard."

"Okay, Hon," I said. "Don't worry about it."

I went outside and was going to pick up that bale and move it, but the wires had rusted and they broke. That big, wet bale of hay was just laying there. What was I going to do then?

I decided to get the wheelbarrow out of the shed, but I saw that its tire had gone flat. So I got our pickup truck and loaded the bale into the back of it.

As I was driving around to the front of the house, Denise came out onto the deck and said, "Where are you going?"

"I'm going to back the truck down the hill beside the house and push the hay into the ravine."

"Don't get stuck," she said.

So I backed up to the ravine and pushed that hay over the edge. I didn't get stuck, even though it had been raining; I stayed right on top of the ground, and that hay just rolled down into the ravine. Then all of that was taken care of.

But when I started to drive the truck forward, it wouldn't go. Its rear tires turned, but it wasn't moving. Then it started to sink.

Soon, all the kids were out on the deck with Denise, leaning over the rail and looking down at me. I could see Denise's mouth moving, as if she were saying, "I told him so! I told him so!"

As I kept working at it, I was getting more frustrated by the minute.

Finally, I said to Denise, "Go get the Suburban and drive it down here!" Then I got a big chain and hooked it to the truck. I said to her, "I'll get that truck out – you just sit behind the wheel and steer it."

I started pushing on the gas in the Suburban and pulling the chain. But then the chain just broke apart!

By this time I was really upset and was covered with sweat. Then it started to rain.

The kids on the deck were saying, "Daddy, can you get it out?"

"No, I can't! Get in the house!" I yelled back.

> **I found out that I still know how to do dumb things, too. That's why you always need to be humble.**

As it turned out, we had to call a wrecker to come and pull that truck out. Since we lived way out in the country, we didn't have wreckers right down the road, so that cost me $90!

When the wrecker came, I was at work, so Denise called to tell me about it. She said, "He got the truck out and it cost us $90, but that's not all."

"What else?" I asked.

"He says you wore out your pressure plate and clutch trying to pull it out of the mud."

"Oh, he doesn't know what he's talking about!" I said. "It can't be ruined; I wasn't doing it that long."

But when I got home, I found out that, sure enough, the truck was shot. No pressure plate. No clutch. It wouldn't move. The engine just made a loud noise.

We really needed that truck, so what were we going to do? Then I said, "I'll call the wrecker and have him to come out and tow it in." Well, that cost me another $90!

It seems that one bale of hay, which had originally cost $2, wound up costing me $424.13!

When I drove the truck home after it was repaired, Sarah and Jessica were on the deck waiting for me. They were looking at one another and just laughing. "Hey, Dad, how much was it?"

"It was enough," I said. "I could have bought a whole barn full of hay for what I've done."

About the time you accuse your kids of doing something, you will wind up doing it yourself. So you have to understand that you are setting an example for them. They are watching you, so they won't be any better stewards over things than you are.

I learned a good lesson through that whole situation. I found out that I still know how to do dumb things, too.

That's why you need to always be humble whenever you're making rules for your kids.

Example Of A Worker Who Had Vision

While I was working for an electrical company, it was my job to hire and train people in manufacturing. We hired young guys right out of high school.

This may be the most important point you get from this study: Most young men don't know where they want to go in life; they just know they want a job. Being right out of high school, it's time for them to go to work.

When starting to work for our company, those guys were paid a good hourly rate, about $2 an hour more than they could make anywhere else in town. They were proud to work there, even though it was hard manual labor.

I remember when some of these guys came in to apply for a job. Some had their shirttails hanging out; some had their shirts unbuttoned down to their bellies, with their sleeves cut off; and some were dipping snuff. They each had to fill out an application, and then I talked with them.

With all of those guys sitting there, another young man walked in. He had just graduated from high school, as those other boys had, only he looked different: he was wearing a white shirt and tie.

He looked different, and he acted different. It seems that his dad worked at a local factory and he was planting the vision inside his kids that God had something good for them.

When this young man came in, he said, "I'd like a job."

After asking his name, I said, "Oh, I don't think we have any jobs you would be looking for."

"I'm looking for any job, even janitor," he said. "I don't care what the job is. I need a job, and I hear you have an opening."

"We do, but you won't be wearing a shirt and tie on this job, Son. This is hard manual labor. It's going to be dirty and greasy."

"I understand that, Sir, and I appreciate it. Can I ask you a question? How much money will I be making five years from now?"

"Son, I don't know how much money *I'll* be making five years from now."

"Well, I just thought I'd like to know if you had a graduated pay scale or what the benefits were."

Then I said, "I'll get you a booklet so that you'll know."

I wound up hiring that young man, and as it turned out, he was a great worker. He showed up early and stayed late, and within eight months was made lead foreman.

Our workers were given two ten-minute breaks on the job, and most of the guys working the big welders would be watching the clock: 3...2...1...BREAK! Then all of them took a break; and when the break was over, those guys would hang around for another two or three minutes, trying to stretch it out.

This young man, on the other hand, hardly ever took a break. He worked through his breaks to get ahead. The other guys didn't like him taking a break anyway because, when he did, he would witness to them about his faith. They didn't want that, so they just let him keep working.

A year later a position for a junior salesman in the front office opened up, so the bosses came to me and said, "We'd like to talk to that kid over there," pointing at the young man. After that, he was moved into the front office.

Before long this man was spending his own time after hours, selling items that had been thrown into the trash bin because we couldn't make a big-enough profit on them. They were by-products of goods we were producing. He would stay there at night, go through the manufacturers' manuals and find companies around the United States that wanted to buy those items. He was making a nice little profit on the side, but the bosses got upset about it, and he almost got fired over it.

Eventually, the young man left and moved to another town. But before he left us, while the other guys were driving to work in their pickup trucks, he was driving a new white T-Bird. He and his wife were living in a nice house.

In his new location, he opened his own business. He eventually started three businesses and had about sixteen men working for him.

Workers With No Vision

Many of the guys I hired at the same time I hired that man are still working there in that shop. That's what I find so amazing about this story. I am making a point here about your kids: The world's system is designed to hold them down and keep them down.

As I said, those guys were being paid $2 an hour more than they could make on some other job. In addition, they were given a free turkey at Thanksgiving, a free ham at Christmas and a $1,200 Christmas bonus. Where else could they get such benefits?

Those guys had much in common: they were all about nineteen years old; they all had girlfriends who thought their guys had the world by the tail; they were all driving new pickup trucks; and they all had hunting dogs and shotguns. As far as they were concerned, life was great.

By getting that $1,200 Christmas bonus, they should have been saving some of it. But as with human nature, most people don't save any of it. They were so thrilled to get it that they were going out and wasting it.

Now for the most part, they were good workers, but they had no vision, no discipline, no idea that God wanted something good to happen in their lives. They didn't really work at getting along with people, and they stayed mad at the company half of the time.

That will bring zero promotion, by the way. If you are griping about your employer, don't expect anything good to happen; God won't let it. If you are badmouthing the place you work, don't look for a raise in your check; it isn't coming. God says you're supposed to be a good employee. If you can't handle it, quit and go to work somewhere else. Until then, pray for favor; pray for that boss who may be mistreating you; do the best job you can, or there will be no promotion.

I know about this. I've been on both sides of the fence.

If nothing is coming your way, you aren't going to force yourself into anything by saying, "Bless God, I'll *make* them give me a raise!" You aren't going to make your boss do anything. If he gave you something, it would be some token gesture. It's not Biblical for you to act that way, and it won't work.

After that young man had been gone for a while, he came back for a visit. It seems he had started contracting out his time because he was so good at what he did. He was making more money than he ever had before. When he came into the office to visit, his pager kept going off, and he kept having to make phone calls. He had also attended a Bible school.

> **What you purpose, God will help you do, but first you have to put your hand to the plow.**

That young man had the same level of education as those other guys, but his dad had planted a vision inside his heart that God had something great planned for him.

Those other guys are making a few bucks more an hour now than they used to make and are still getting that $1,200 bonus. The problem is, now their pickups are beaten to a pulp and their hunting dogs have died. Their girlfriends became their wives, and they have two or three kids; but they're still just trying to make ends meet.

Proverbs 29:18 says, **"Where there is no vision, the people perish."**

A Good Work Ethic

Now in training our high-school students, I would tell them: "People are going to be interviewing you for a job, even if it's to work at a fast-food restaurant; and I'll tell you what they're looking for right now." Then I would explain how they should look and act during an interview.

You know, more kids today are going on for a college education. As Scripture says, **"The wealth of the wicked is laid up for the just"** (Proverbs 13:22).

You may say, "Well, we can't afford to send our kids to college." But you can. Money is everywhere, and the diligent will get it.

Each year, people from the College Board SAT Program would come to our city and hold an informative seminar for administrators and guidance counselors to let us know what changes had been made on the college entrance exams.

One of the representatives made the astounding comment that colleges and industries were no longer looking for trained young people, but for *trainable* young people. He told us that knowledge was exploding all over the earth and that there was enough new information going into the Library of Congress each hour to fill up five sets of encyclopedias. He said with technology increasing as it is, even if a person received a degree, eighteen months after he finished school it might be obsolete. We always need to be learning.

The Bible says that **the hand of the diligent (the hardworking one) will bear rule and will be made rich** (Proverbs 12:24; 10:4). So whether our children attend college, receive vocational training, enter the military or start work on the ground floor of a company, God's will is for them to succeed.

What you purpose, God will help you do. The Holy Spirit will be your Helper, but first you have to put your hand to the plow. You can't just wish you had a plow; you have to find a plow and place your hand on it. Even if you don't like that particular plow, you have to keep plowing with it until you get a better one. Plow well with the one you have and take care of it, because if you are faithful with it, you will get another one.

You have to put into your children the idea that they don't start at the top; they start at the bottom. If they started at the top, it wouldn't last long. If they can get there that quickly, then they can leave there just as quickly. They have to start at the bottom, apply themselves and be good stewards. They have to show up on time and do what they're supposed to do and then do even above that.

I promise you, if an unbeliever could say of Daniel, "we perceive an excellent spirit in this young man, so let's put him in charge," that employer you have, who complains all the time, can put you in charge, too. As acts 10:34 says, **"God is no respecter of persons."** We just have to do our jobs. And, as parents, we have to place that work ethic inside our children.

Always Work *With* God, Not *Without* Him

At church, we hear about how we're to win the world. We're to go out and tell the world how good God is and show them His goodness by living a blessed life that is led by Him.

Do you believe in God? Are you praying? That's how you are going to be led. I wouldn't want to go through life without the Holy Spirit leading and guiding me. But **"faith without works is dead"** (James 2:26), so we have to have both faith and works to succeed.

If you're going to work without God, you can work yourself into an early grave.

I've seen this happen to family members and friends. It really hurts, but it's a real eye-opener.

When I stand before God with my children, I want Him to look at all six of them and say to each one: "Well done, thou good and faithful servant." I want Him to say that, not because they're perfect, but because they kept getting back up every time they had fallen. It goes back to our being righteous.

I want my kids to know what God is saying to them, so I tell them: "Look, just because you bit the dust doesn't change God's plan. Things may not look good now, but He still has the plans. I want you to know you have to obey the authority God places in your life. You can't kick at authority all the time and get anywhere. You have to understand that you're gifted to succeed at something. All you have to do is find out what that something is and then get after it. Start stewarding the little part of it, and it will begin to grow. God will begin to add to it as you are able to handle it."

Then I tell them, "And you had better know how to get along with people."

You can have the greatest vision and be the most self-disciplined and most gifted individual in the world. But if you can't get along with people, nobody will give you the time of day, because they don't want to be around you.

So you have to teach your kids how to steward what God has given them and how to get along with people, both their friends and their enemies. They have to learn to walk with wisdom toward everyone.

Pray this prayer as parents and as God's stewards of your home:

> *Father, we thank You for the cleansing blood of Jesus Christ. We thank You that we have the ability to come to You boldly and confess our sins, and You are faithful and just to forgive us and cleanse us.*
>
> *We are not known as the perfect people, but as the "getting back up" people. I thank You that we will get up and dust ourselves off, repent and put our hands to the plow and set ourselves to do great things for You, Father.*
>
> *As parents, we commit to growing and setting a godly example for our children through Your Word and Your Spirit. I thank You that we are wise stewards over what You've given us.*
>
> *I say now by faith that our children will do great things, Father. We don't see them as they are today; we see them as what they will become. And we, as parents, will be the biggest cheerleaders in our home.*

Father, I ask in Jesus' name that You teach my children to fear You (according to Psalm 34:11), that you surround them with a shield of divine favor (Psalm 5:12), and that you bring godly friends into their lives (Proverbs 27:17). Thank You, Lord. Amen.

CHAPTER 12

Favor With Man = Friendship

And Jesus increased in wisdom and stature, and in favour
with God and man.

Luke 2:52

Thus far in our study, we have looked at the subjects of *vision*,
discipline and *stewardship*. Now let's consider the fourth part of this
verse:

And Jesus increased ... *in favour with ... man.*

Now regarding this phrase, *favor with man,* immediately you may
wonder if you've really read the New Testament. You might
wonder, how could Jesus have had favor with man? He faced
challenges constantly, having to deal with the Sadducees, the
Pharisees and the mobs of people who tried to stone Him or throw
Him over a cliff. But Jesus just walked through the midst of them
(John 8:59; 10:31, 39; Luke 4:28-30).

Scripture doesn't say, "Jesus had favor with man and therefore was loved by everybody." He knew how to deal not only with His friends but with His enemies. Sometimes He even got on to His best friends. He raised His voice with them because He loved them and wanted to see them change. He would admonish them and encourage them.

The key word we will use for *favor with man* is *friendship*.

After discussing friendship in general, I will give you some information about teaching your children how to pick their friends and how to get into a dating relationship. God is big on people getting together, but there are some guidelines we need to follow. Then we will look into the subject of how to teach your children about sex. It will be good, and I will give you some recommended reading.

Show Yourself Friendly

> A man that hath friends must show himself friendly....
>
> Proverbs 18:24

Friends don't appear out of nowhere. The only way you will ever have friends in this life is by showing yourself friendly. God won't just look down someday, feel sorry for you and send lots of friends your way because you're lonely. If you don't show yourself friendly, you'll never have any friends.

One time I was counseling a man who had been in America for about two years after leaving his family in another country. He was crying, and when I asked what his problem was, he said, "I have no friends."

"Where are your friends?" I asked.

"They have all moved away."

As we talked, he kept repeating himself. I don't know what he thought I was going to be able to do, maybe sprinkle some magic dust on him, open the closet door and have somebody just jump out and become his friend.

I kept trying to tell him how to fix the problem. I said: "There are places where people gather together, so if you want friends, you have to go where they are. It takes being around people first before you can have a friend." For a while it was a struggle to teach him how to be friendly.

If you go into a room full of people, they aren't just going to run up to you and clamor over you. If you want friends, you have to show yourself friendly.

This is the Golden Rule: *Do unto others as you would have them do unto you.* Jesus said it this way:

> Therefore all things whatsoever ye would that men should do to you, do ye even so to them....
>
> Matthew 7:12

A Real Friend

There are more scriptures in the Bible having to do with friends than with Hell. Just look up the words in a concordance and count all those references. The topic of Hell is important, and we all should want to avoid going there, but there is more to be said in God's Word about friendship. Any person, including a child, will become like the people he hangs out with.

David Wilkerson, author of *The Cross And The Switchblade* (New York, NY: Jove Books, 1977), wrote another book entitled *Parents On Trial* (New York, NY: Pyramid Books, 1970). In it he shares questions he asked each of the teens in his Teen Challenge program. Their conversation went something like this:

"How did you end up in this mess? How did you get involved with things like drugs, vandalism, pornography and prostitution?"

Without exception, they all said, "We began to hang out with the wrong crowd."

When he asked them how they got their first snort of dope, they answered, "A friend gave it to me."

"How did you first get into stealing?"

"A friend took me along."

> **We will have lots of acquaintances in this life but very few real friends.**

Let me tell you something, Mom and Dad: No matter how many times your kids go through the doors of a church or how many times you make them memorize Scripture, they will become like those they hang out with.

We won't have many *real* friends, and neither will our kids. We will have lots of acquaintances in this life but very few real friends. We may have one, two, maybe three, in our whole lifetime. A real friend is somebody who would lay down his life for us. We need to teach this truth to our children.

As we learned in a previous chapter, a good friend will sharpen us like iron. Scripture says:

> Iron sharpeneth iron; so a man sharpeneth the countenance of his friend.
>
> Proverbs 27:17

Do you know what happens when you strike iron?

The sparks will fly. Good friendships will cause some sparks to fly. But that's what keeps them sharp.

A real friend will tell you the truth – how you have bad breath or dandruff, or are getting a little pudgy around the middle. Your friend will tell you the truth because he loves you.

An acquaintance won't necessarily tell you the truth. He may just mush you up and then mess you up.

The Value Of Christian Training

In the book, *Growing Up God's Way* by John A. Stormer (Florrisant, MO: Liberty Bell Press, 1984), we find a story that illustrates the value of Christian training in the home.

In 1874 the state of New York had a terrible problem. Its prisons were overcrowded, and new facilities couldn't be built fast enough. The state officials didn't know what to do. So a man named R.A. Dugdale was hired to do some research. He came back with a fascinating report. (I have no idea about Dugdale's spiritual condition. There is nothing in the history books to give us any indication about that.)

Dugdale did a study of two families and their descendants over some six generations to see how the different lifestyles affected their children.

The first half of his report was about a family named Jukes. Both Max Jukes and his brother married sisters. According to the report, neither of them believed in Christian training. (I don't know the details of what was meant by "Christian training.")

They had 1,026 descendants. Because of their lifestyles, 300 of them died young and many others suffered poor health. Among the descendants, 140 served an average of 13 years each in prison, 190 were confirmed public prostitutes and 100 were alcoholics. Over a 100-year period this family cost the state of New York $1.2 million.

The second half of the report compared the Jukes family with another family named Edwards. Jonathan Edwards, whom you might remember from your history books, was a Christian minister who married a girl "of like belief."

Edwards and his wife had 729 descendants. Of those, 300 were preachers, 65 were college professors, 13 were university presidents, 60 were authors, 3 were congressman and 1 served as Vice-President of the United States. With the exception of a grandson named Aaron Burr, who was hanged, this second family cost the state of New York not one single penny.

The difference in these two families was that one family believed in Christian training while the other just raised up their kids and fed them.

Our Children Are Our Reward

> Lo, children are an heritage of the Lord: and the fruit of the womb is his reward.
>
> Psalm 127:3

Our kids will be our reward. Whether that reward is good or bad will be determined by what we do with them. If we feel called to save this world and preach the Gospel to the lost, then we had better be serious about teaching and training our children to follow after God each day of their lives.

Scripture doesn't say parents have to be so somber that we never laugh. I believe in laughter as an expression of the joy of the Lord (Psalm 126:2).

Sometimes Christians look as if they've been sucking on sour pickles! Instead of giving a testimony of what God has done for them, they're always talking about how bad their lives were the day before.

But as the Bible says: **"Let the redeemed of the Lord say so. Let the weak say, I am strong, and the poor say, I am rich"** (Psalm 107:2, Joel 3:10, Proverbs 10:22).

If you keep hanging around the wrong kind of people, you will think just like they think.

Again, Proverbs 18:24 says, **"A man that hath friends must show himself friendly...."** Our children aren't going to grow up and automatically be friendly. It's a skill they have to be taught. To make friends, they must be taught certain social skills, such as how to carry on a conversation.

Let me give you one way I have worked at training my kids to talk to other people.

The Elevator Game

When being introduced to someone, I have noticed that, instead of looking in my direction, some people will stare down as if something was just dropped on the ground. How are they ever going to win the world for Jesus if they can't even look another person in the face?

> **Our children aren't going to grow up and automatically be friendly. It's a skill they have to be taught.**

Having traveled around the country, I have stayed in lots of big hotels. I remember how intimidated I once was when riding on an elevator with strangers.

As an example, let's say you get on an elevator at the 28th floor going down to the hotel lobby. If another person gets on when you do, you both stare up at the floor number as if it's so fascinating to watch it change for those 27 floors.

I determined that I wasn't going to do that anymore. So I learned to play what I call the elevator game. Now it drives my kids nuts to get on an elevator with me. That's when I get tenacious. It even scares some people.

As a young boy I was afraid to meet people or to get up in front of a class at school. When you're a scared little boy, you aren't going anywhere. Scared people will never have anything and will never get anywhere. Proverbs 28:1 says, "**... The righteous are bold as a lion.**"

So now whenever I get on an elevator with a stranger, the first thing I do, even before the door closes, is start talking. I ask people questions like: "What's your name? What are you doing here? Are you on vacation? Have you ever been here before? What is there to see around this area?"

I don't always know what to say; I just open my mouth and start talking.

I would practice the elevator game with the kids at school and with my kids at home on Saturday morning. My kids didn't really like playing that game, so they would always say, "Oh, Dad, not this morning – please." But that didn't stop me.

Selecting one of them to be the contestant, I'd say, "Come on… stand up." I looked at my watch and said, "You have five minutes to talk, and there's a penalty if you don't go that long." Then I gave them a subject to talk about. The moment I said, "Go," they had to start talking to me and just keep talking until I told them to stop.

As an example, let's say I picked tennis shoes as the subject. When I said, "Go," that kid would begin talking, sounding something like this: "I like tennis shoes. I have a pair; in fact, I have several pairs. Tennis shoes are made in several different colors. Some of mine are worn out. I don't have any shoestrings in them right now, but I'm going to get some shoestrings. I use my tennis shoes to run and to play basketball. Sometimes I don't know where they are, and I have to look for them. Sometimes my mom yells at me because I don't know where they are. I even lost a pair of them one time. They sure cost a lot of money – $85.95 a pair!"

Do you get the idea? You might want to try it with your kids.

Teach Your Kids To Be Friendly

Strongly encourage your kids to speak up, to look people in the eye and to shake hands with them. Most businessmen say that they can tell how a business deal will go with a person by the way that person shakes hands.

Children need to learn how to be friendly. It's a skill, but they can learn it. Anybody can learn it.

But if our kids don't ever learn to be friendly, they will be susceptible to the first person who shows any sign of affection toward them. Somebody will be trying to draw from our kids, but I don't want anybody except me drawing anything out of my children. That's my job as a parent.

Make Sure Your Friend

Proverbs 27:10 says, **"Thine own friend, and thy father's friend, forsake not...."** Just because you had a friend once doesn't mean that person will stay your friend forever. You have to "make sure," or secure, that friend.

Friends don't just automatically stay friends. They don't become card-carrying members of the Friendship Club and say, "You're my friend forever, even if I never talk to you again." That isn't how it works.

If you intend to keep a friend, you have to do as the Bible says: continually show yourself friendly and make sure your friend.

Think about it: Have you sent your friend a card lately or given your friend a call or taken your friend out to eat? Why don't you run over to your friend's house and see if you can be of help with something? There will come a day when you will have need of a friend, maybe even a lot of friends. It's always good to have friends.

A Friend Can Be Your Closest Companion

A friend loveth at all times, and a brother is born for adversity.

Proverbs 17:17

Sometimes your closest companion won't be somebody of your own blood, but a friend. That's hard for some people to believe, but it's the truth.

Let's look again at Proverbs 27:17, which says, **"Iron sharpeneth iron; so a man sharpeneth the countenance of his friend."** A good friend will sharpen you and make you a better person.

> **Children are the most susceptible to flattery when they aren't receiving praise at home.**

When iron sharpens iron, sparks fly. That means true friends will be honest with you and will always tell you the truth. If you just want people to lie to you, you don't need a real friend; you just need to be surrounded by a bunch of people.

The Bible teaches us to mark those given to flattery. As Scripture says:

> To flatter friends is to lay a trap for their feet.
>
> Evil people are trapped by sin, but the righteous escape, shouting for joy.
> Proverbs 29:5, 6 NLT
>
> He that goeth about as a talebearer revealeth secrets: therefore meddle not with him that flattereth with his lips.
> Proverbs 20:19

You need to teach your children about flattery. Children are the most susceptible to flattery when they aren't receiving any praise at home. The degree to which someone flatters you to your face is the degree to which they can plunge a knife into your back. Teach your kids to watch out for flattery. It's just a lot of cheap words.

Friendship is so important. I wanted my children to have good friends. One of the most important things I prayed every day is for my kids to find good friends. My prayer went something like this:

Father, I thank You for giving my children godly friends, those who will sharpen them like iron. Send my children some good friends who will sharpen them and keep them sharp. If You have to, move those good friends in from another state. I pray that if any of their friends won't sharpen them You will just remove them out of the way.

This sounds strong until you see the results of poor friendships. Your child's poor selection of friends can be devastating.

This is a good prayer for you to pray, too. Just thank God every day that your kids will have good friends.

We Cannot Survive Alone

Two are better than one; because they have a good reward for their labour.

For if they fall, the one will lift up his fellow: but woe to him that is alone when he falleth; for he hath not another to help him up.

Ecclesiastes 4:9, 10

Verse 12 says:

...and a threefold cord is not quickly broken.

In other words, this means the more the merrier; we cannot survive alone.

That's why the Bible says:

Let us consider one another to provoke unto love and to good works:

Not forsaking the assembling of ourselves together, as the manner of some is; but exhorting one another: and so much the more, as ye see the day approaching.

Hebrews 10:24, 25 (Author's emphasis)

There will be times when you are to be a blessing to others and they are to be a blessing to you. It's a mutual benefit set up by God.

As believers, we are not to forsake the assembling of ourselves together in these Last Days. God's people need one another. We need more than ever to be involved somewhere in church – in a youth group, in children's church, in an adult Bible study. We need to be with fellow believers. We are commanded to come together in the name of the Lord. We need one another; we cannot survive alone.

Don't get out there by yourself and be isolated. You must realize that there are no perfect people, no perfect families, no perfect kids. But there are strong people, strong families and strong kids. Not perfect but strong through God.

Righteous people bite the dust on a regular basis. What are you to do when you fall to the ground? Get up, spit the rocks and dirt out of your mouth, dust yourself off, repent to God, put your hand back on the plow and start moving again.

Remember, every chance he gets, the devil will come at you with guilt. He'll make you feel bad about what you've done or failed to do as a parent. He will make you think that life is just made for hanging on and surviving. But God says you can thrive.

Don't Be The Friend Of An Angry Man

> Make no friendship with an angry man; and with a furious man thou shalt not go:
>
> Lest thou learn his ways, and get a snare to thy soul.
> Proverbs 22:24, 25

If you hang around someone who is always losing his temper, you'll begin to think that's how you should act. You'll think that by losing your temper you will get what you want. But how you react to situations will label you.

I don't want to learn the ways of an angry person. I don't want to be around anyone who can't control himself. If you can't control yourself, you'll end up hurting somebody. I would swing a wide path around someone like that.

Be Careful When Picking Close Friends

As Scripture says, **"Don't be deceived, for evil associations will corrupt good manners"** (Author's paraphrase; 1 Corinthians 15:33). You can have a good child who has good morals and has been taught good manners, but evil associations will corrupt him.

Proverbs 14:7 says:

> Go from the presence of a foolish man, when thou perceivest not in him the lips of knowledge.

How do you tell your children who to stay away from and who to get close to?

We are commanded by God to love every single person on this planet. There is no option. As I tell my kids: "You are commanded in the Word of God to love everybody – whatever the situation. If somebody is thirsty, give him some water. If he's hungry, feed him. If he's in the hospital or prison, go visit him. If his car is stuck in a ditch, help pull him out. If he's moving away, help load the truck."

But when it comes to friendships – the people we spend our spare time with – God is very specific. Doing things for other people doesn't mean we're obligated to sit down and have lunch with them. We're not required to spend our spare time with them. We have to teach our kids this truth.

There are 22 traits given in the Bible that we really ought to watch out for in people. Let's look at this passage:

> This know also, that in the last days perilous times shall come.

For men shall be lovers of their own selves, covetous, boasters, proud, blasphemers, disobedient to parents, unthankful *(which is why we need to teach our kids to say thank you)*, unholy,

Without natural affection, trucebreakers, false accusers, incontinent, fierce, despisers of those that are good *(which covers the media making fun of God's people)*,

Traitors, heady, highminded, lovers of pleasures more than lovers of God;

Having a form of godliness, but denying the power thereof: from such turn away.
> 2 Timothy 3:1-5 (Author's paraphrase; vv. 2, 3)

This passage tells us to stay away from people like this. We don't have to hang around them.

You might say, "But I thought Christians are to love everybody."

Yes, that's what the Bible says, but that doesn't mean we have to sit down and become friends with everybody. If you're hungry, I'll feed you, but I'm not automatically going to spend my spare time with you.

Kids Should Be Cautious Around Strangers

Sometimes children are taught to be friendly to everybody. But I don't want my children to be friendly to just anybody, and I taught them that. There are some people my kids should avoid.

I remember once when an old friend was visiting in town. He was a real back-patting kind of guy. But when he reached over to hug one of my daughters, she politely but firmly said, "Please don't touch me." He was a good guy, but kids don't always know that.

My kids have been taught how certain people may try to take advantage of others. We've heard about child abductions – how some stranger, being really friendly, will come up to a kid and ask for directions. I warned my kids to watch out for that. They didn't have any fear about it; they just had knowledge.

As God's Word says, **"My people are destroyed for lack of knowledge"** (Hosea 4:6). We can be friendly when we know the boundaries. Instead of hiding in a hole and being scared about everything, we can have knowledge of the Word. **"So then faith cometh by hearing, and hearing by the word of God"** (Romans 10:17). We are to do everything we know to do; then God will do the rest. He is faithful.

Disrespectful Of Parents

One of the traits mentioned in 2 Timothy 3, is disobedience to parents.

We were very careful not to let kids come into our house and start talking trash about their moms and dads. When they did this, we would quickly correct them. If they continued to dishonor their parents, that was the last time they would be invited to our home. I didn't want my kids around those who were running down their parents.

Ephesians 6:2, 3 says, **"Honour thy father and mother... That it may be well with thee, and thou mayest live long on the earth."** When kids are showing dishonor toward their moms and dads, they will pay a price for it in this life. I didn't want my children learning their ways.

Listening To Bad Talk From Kids At School

We also have to teach our children how to handle certain traits in other people. Our kids can be caught in some compromising situations.

They might be hanging around other kids in the hall at school when all of a sudden those kids start talking trash. If our kids don't back away immediately, they may find themselves laughing along with the rest of them at something they shouldn't be laughing at and sounding like a bunch of hyenas.

Our kids can see if the conversation isn't going anywhere. They don't have to make a big religious scene out of it. They don't have to stay there and condemn the other kids by preaching to them, either. They just need to ease on down the hall, saying, "Well, it's time to go; I have to get to class."

Proverbs 14:7 says, **"Go from the presence of a foolish man, when thou perceivest not in him the lips of knowledge."**

With wisdom, our children can avoid embarrassing situations. We need to teach our children how to back out of those situations and not get caught up in them.

Finally, a life-changing experience would be for a family to get a concordance and a Bible, to look up Scripture verses on the subject of friends and friendship and to write them out by hand. You and your family will never be the same. You can't have a friend until you know how to be one.

Let's look next into the subject of dating. Now that we know how to choose our friends, it will help in the process of choosing a lifetime mate. After all, your spouse should be your best friend.

CHAPTER 13

This Dating Thing

The whole idea behind friendship is that our kids will eventually get into dating.

Every person yearns for love, and most look for it in marriage. More than ninety percent of all the people in the United States will marry at least once in their lifetime. But each year in the United States, more than 200,000 marriages end prior to the couple's second anniversary, mostly because they decided too quickly, were too young and had unrealistic expectations.

The number of unmarried teenagers getting pregnant has nearly doubled in the past few decades. Though rare in the early 1960s, by the late 1980s nearly one in ten unmarried teenage girls got pregnant. According to the American Enterprise Institute (www.aei.org), teenage sexual activity now results in nearly one million pregnancies annually.

Most of the young people we have counseled in this area are born-again, Spirit-filled, church-going Christians, so there must be something wrong. Why are they having to deal with these problems?

Kids Don't Relate To Their Parents' Past

Listen to this carefully, Mom and Dad: God's Word doesn't say He will watch over *your* testimony to perform it; it says He will watch over *His Word* to perform it (Jeremiah 1:12 AMP). We really don't have any business telling our kids about what we did or didn't do as young people. Once we've repented, it's nobody's business what we repented of. According to Scripture, the moment we repented, God took our transgressions as far as the east is from the west and cast them into the depths of the sea (Psalm 103:12, Micah 7:19).

> **We really don't have any business telling our kids what we did or didn't do as young people.**

As I mentioned earlier, I married my childhood sweetheart. Denise is the first girl I dated and the first girl I kissed. A year and a half later, we were married. But not everyone is that way.

You can't just tell your kids, "You're going to be like your mother and me." God may have a different set of steps for them.

You don't have to share everything about your past life with your kids, thinking it will help them in some way. As Scripture says, God watches over *His Word* to perform it – not your life story. I do believe in sharing the great things God has done, passing on the faith to the next generation, but my former life as a sinner gives no glory to God; neither does it build faith in my children. So, instead, let's tell them what the Word says.

Kids Who Think They're In Love

One day while in the middle of a class at school, I noticed two high school students sitting there. I could see they were "in love."

Having swapped rings, they had that lovesick look about them. She was wearing his ring on her finger with lots of masking tape wrapped around it, and he wore hers on a little chain around his neck. During the chapel service, they were sitting close to one another, closer than they were supposed to.

I shouldn't have done this, but I called them out and said, "I want the two of you to stand up for a minute. You must really be in love. This is getting serious, isn't it?"

The guy just stood there like a tree stump. I said a few more things, then finally the girl fired back at me, "That's right, Mr. McGee. We're planning to get married."

When she said that, his eyes widened just a bit. I could see that his buddies were snickering and making comments among themselves. His ship was slowly sinking. Obviously, he hadn't seen the relationship progressing quite as far as she had.

Then I said, "I'm really impressed that you two young people can make such a mature decision at such a young age. That's difficult for a lot of young people to do. I know you love God and His Word. The Bible has so many scriptures on friendship, and I know you've based your relationship on the Word of God. Would you please tell me one of those scriptures on friendship that your relationship is based on?"

Again, the guy just stared at me. He wasn't really listening; he just looked scared.

Finally, the girl thought up a scripture and spoke out in a questioning tone, "A friend sticketh closer than a brother?"

"Okay, you can sit down," I said.

It seems too often these days that young people think they're in love when they can't even spell the word!

The typical thing is for the guy to drive up in front of his girl's house in his souped-up car or his daddy's clunker (whichever he can get) and blow the horn, and the girl starts toward the door.

"Where are you going?" her daddy asks.

"Out," she says.

"Really? Where?"

"Oh, just out," she responds.

Wrong Answer!

I'd say, "If you don't know where you're going, you might get lost, so you can just stay right here."

An Assignment For My Students

As I mentioned earlier, every year I taught a course to our seniors on developing a biblical world view. At the beginning of the year I had them select a subject to investigate. They chose subjects such as crime, the economy, abortion, sports and money.

Then I would say: "For the next quarter I want you to look through the newspaper every weekday, find an article on that subject, cut it out and put it in a scrapbook. At the end of the quarter you're to write a summary paper, based on those 45 articles, telling what has been going on with that subject and what the world says about it.

"Next, I want you to take your concordance and your Bible, look up 25 scriptures about your subject and find out what God has to say about it. Then you are to get up in front of the class and in five minutes tell us the difference between those two views based on your research.

"I don't care what subject you pick. Whatever the world has been saying about that subject for the past nine weeks, God has been saying exactly the opposite for the last 2,000 years. The world is at enmity with God. He is at the opposite end of the scale from the world.

Along with that scrapbook, they kept a second scrapbook which included information from the newspaper on births, deaths, marriages, divorces and drunk drivers. For the first week, all they did was find names people gave to their new babies. It was kind of cute for those first few days.

Then the second week I said: "Now we're going to do something different. I want you to look down through the list of new births from all the hospitals and see how many moms are listed as giving birth to a baby without the daddy's name being given, implying a single mother who has given birth."

In a school year, we found that in our city 33 percent of the time the dad's name was never listed next to the mother's.

Then I said: "Now, let's pick out one of these mothers. Here's a girl named Jennifer. It says she had a little baby girl yesterday, but the daddy's name isn't mentioned here in the paper. Where do you suppose he is this morning?"

> **Whatever the world has been saying about a subject, God has been saying exactly the opposite.**

Those kids just looked at me.

I said: "Think about it. He's probably at home with his own mother this morning eating cereal, while Mom does his laundry and everything else for him. Then later on today, he'll probably hang around with the guys and shoot some hoops. But Jennifer won't be going out and doing any of those fun things; she has a newborn baby to take care of."

After nine months of cutting out this information from the newspapers, several girls told me how they felt about it. One said: "Mr. McGee, when I was out on a date the other night, that guy was really giving me a line. But, you know, all I could see was that section of the newspaper showing how those mothers gave birth to little babies with no support from the daddies."

The Story Of Two Bald Eagles

I want to give you a story that I always tell teenagers when I talk about dating and courtship. This story is about bald eagles and how they mate. There are lots of bald eagles in our part of the state of Oklahoma, down on the river.

The bald eagle has a unique mating ritual. To appreciate the story, you have to understand that female bald eagles are always bigger than males. That's just a fact of nature.

In the story I tell, there are two eagles, a female and a male. To add a personal touch, I give them names: Ernestine is the female and Ernie is the male.

Ernestine gets up one morning and, like eagles do every morning, she goes out flying, looking for some food. Then Ernie sees her flying up high, so he comes up right behind her and says, "Wow, Ernestine, you're looking good today!" She looks around, sees him looking at her and realizes that he is making a move for her.

She flies down to the river bank and picks up a little stick. Then she takes it back up and begins a figure-eight movement in the air. She works at building up speed, and when she hits maximum speed, she lets go of that stick.

Being the gentleman that he is, Ernie dives for the stick, grabs it and brings it back to her. But Ernestine won't take it.

She flies back down to the river bank, and gets a bigger stick, carries it up and starts the figure-eight again, building up speed.

Ernie is behind her again, yelling out, "Ernestine, you're looking good!"

When Ernestine hits maximum speed, she lets go of the stick. Again being the gentleman, Ernie dives for it, grabs it and brings it back to her. But again she refuses it.

Ernestine repeats this process over and over. It's said that a mature female bald eagle can pick up the equivalent of an eight-foot fence post.

Again, Ernestine flies down to the river bank, this time picking up a small log and stirring the dust as she gets it off the ground. She takes it up about five-hundred feet, starts the figure-eight and builds up speed.

Ernie, flying right behind her, is thinking, *What a female I've found!*

But this time, when Ernestine lets go of that log and Ernie takes off after it, he doesn't realize that he is now past the point of no return. Male eagles have been known to die trying to catch that log. Some of them snap their wings trying to stop it, others fly straight into the water, while still others hit the ground with a thud.

If Ernie, realizing he can't stop the log before it hits the ground, chickens out and lets go of it, then Ernestine will dive down, attack him and either run him off or kill him in a fight.

If Ernie had been able to stop that log and hold it there, even momentarily, Ernestine would then have mated with him for life. Here's why: Come late winter or early spring when she's sitting in the nest on top of those eggs and, early one cold morning, the snow is hitting her in the face, she wants to know beforehand, not afterward, that Ernie will be capable of bringing home the "bacon" that morning.

Too Close Too Soon

Sexual intercourse does not just happen; it is a result of choices that are made. There are several steps leading up to sexual intercourse, step one usually being that of holding hands, followed by a series of other steps.

In their book *Too Close Too Soon* (Nashville, TN: Thomas Nelson, 1982), Jim Talley and Bobbie Reed estimate that it takes a boy and a girl about 300 hours of spending time alone together before their relationship develops from casual acquaintance to a sexually active involvement. That means if they go out on a date every Friday and Saturday night for four to five hours each night, it will take them about seven months to reach that point. **Too close too soon!**

One day in November many years ago a young couple came to my office at school, knocked on my door and said, "Mr. McGee, can we see you?"

> **Sexual intercourse does not just happen; it is a result of choices that are made.**

Both of them were seniors, and they planned to be married the following June. They were born again and Spirit-filled, as were their parents, and everybody seemed to be in agreement about the marriage.

"Come on in," I said. "Have a seat."

They sat down and then just stared at me. He took a deep breath, and then tears came into her eyes.

"Is there a problem?" I asked.

"Yes, Mr. McGee, we need some help."

They just sat there and stared at me some more. Then it dawned on me what the problem might be.

"Have you two committed fornication?" I asked.

The young man's eyes opened wide, and he drew a deep breath. Then he said, "No, Sir, we haven't."

But she added, "We've come awfully close though." Then she began to cry and said, "We're concerned and scared. We think we're seeing too much of one another."

"Well, what do you want me to do?" I asked.

"We don't know, Mr. McGee. We think maybe we need to break up for about three months and just not see one another. What do you think?"

"I think that's probably a good idea."

It's amazing what kids will do sometimes when they have heard the Word of God. They will do what they have heard. They came to me for some advice and some wisdom, so I said: "I'll tell you what we'll do: I'll call your parents and have them come down here. Then I want you to repeat to them what you just told me. I can promise you, they'll help you stay apart for the next three months."

And they did stay apart. Then when June came, they didn't get married; instead, they were married in August of that year.

Today they are the parents of some beautiful children, and both of them are working in the church. I still see them from time to time, and I think, *Great couple! Great marriage!* But there is a unique twist to this story: They didn't marry each other! They came very close, but they each married someone else that August!

I've had kids sit in my office and say, "I just did it once, Mr. McGee. Honest to God, just once!"

I would say, "I understand; but if you sow human seed, you will reap human crop." That's just a natural, biological law.

The world today is trying to do something with the problems of sexual promiscuity and the abundance of babies being born to young people. But they want to fix it by working on steps eleven and twelve. Unfortunately, it can't be done that way. We have to go back to the beginning and start working at step number one.

God Warns Against Sin

In Jeremiah 29, there are some principles we will look at which I think can be used to relate to dating and its pattern.

If you read back in Scripture, you will see that the prophet Jeremiah knew the people of Israel would be going away for seventy years. They had been sinning, and God had warned them many times through the prophet, saying, "If you don't repent, judgment is coming." But they refused to repent.

So God spoke through Jeremiah to a group of teenage boys who were being carried away captive out of Jerusalem to Babylon. In effect, He was saying to them: "Gentlemen, you're going on a little trip, and you won't be back for seventy years. But I'll tell you how you can handle your life over the next seventy years and prosper."

God is merciful, longsuffering and very forgiving. He will warn His people forever and a day before something happens.

God's Warning To Nineveh

That's exactly what we see in the book of Jonah. God told Jonah to go and warn the people of Nineveh that they needed to quit sinning (Jonah 1:2). But Jonah didn't want to go. He was probably thinking, *If I go over there, those wicked people are going to repent,* but he didn't want them to repent.

Those people had done some really bad things, but God didn't want to kill them; He wanted them to stop sinning. All God ever wants people to do is to stop sinning.

Jonah went in a direction that was different from God's instruction and, as a result, he was taken in the belly of a whale, or great fish, and dumped onto the shore. Again, God told him to go to Nineveh and preach His message (Jonah 3:1). Finally, Jonah got there. I think he probably gave some wimpy little sermon, telling the people, "You had better quit all of that sin!"

The Bible tells how all the people – from the king down to the least of the nation – repented in sackcloth and ashes (Jonah 3:5-10). God didn't send judgment on them for another four-hundred years. Is that long-suffering, or what? God is merciful. All He wants is for people to repent and stop sinning.

The Man Of God Speaks

Then one day, as mentioned in the book of Jeremiah, King Nebuchadnezzar and the Babylonians in all their fury came against Israel. They were killing, pillaging and burning. Things were bad. When the day was over, not many people were left and Jerusalem was on fire.

> **God is merciful. All He wants is for people to repent and stop sinning.**

When this occurred, a group of teenage boys, thought to be the smartest, best looking and most prominent in the community, were gathered up and taken hostage. Among them were Daniel, Shadrach, Meshach and Abednego. (See Daniel 1:1-7.)

Then Jeremiah the prophet sent a letter to the boys when they were in prison.

Here's what it said:

> Thus saith the Lord of hosts, the God of Israel, unto all that are carried away captives, whom I have caused to be carried away from Jerusalem unto Babylon;
>
> Build ye houses…
>
> Jeremiah 29:4, 5

About this time Shadrach probably looked over at Daniel and said, "What did that old man say?"

Daniel said, "I think he said something about building a house."

Seven Points To Dating

Let's read on in this passage of Scripture. Then I will break it down and comment as we go.

> Build ye houses, and dwell in them; and plant gardens, and eat the fruit of them;
>
> Take ye wives, and beget sons and daughters; and take wives for your sons, and give your daughters to husbands, that they may bear sons and daughters; that ye may be increased there, and not diminished.
>
> And seek the peace of the city whither I have caused you to be carried away captives, and pray unto the Lord for it: for in the peace thereof shall ye have peace.
>
> Jeremiah 29:5-7

I see in this passage of Scripture a list of seven points to dating and getting married. In paraphrasing, here's what the prophet was saying:

Step # 1: *Build a house.* In other words, get yourself a place to live; you won't be living with your mama.

Step # 2: *Dwell in it.* In other words, set up housekeeping. You need things like furniture to sit on and to eat off of; eating utensils like plates, cups, knives, forks and spoons; and everyday household items like toilet paper, toothpaste and light bulbs.

Step # 3: *Plant a garden.* Paraphrasing from the agricultural society, to me that's saying, *Get a job!* In order for you to have a place to live and a house to keep up, you must get a job.

Step # 4: *Eat the fruit of it.* Can you eat what you are growing? In other words, can you keep that job? Will it sustain you? Is it working for you?

Once you have those basics – a place in which to live, a house to keep up and a job that will pay your living expenses – then you can go on to the next step.

Step # 5: *Take a wife (or husband).* In other words, find yourself a girlfriend (or boyfriend) and then get married.

Step # 6: *Now you can have a baby.* These days too many people jump straight to step six. We will be looking into this aspect of life in further detail, but first let's complete the list with the last step.

Step # 7: *Pray for God's peace in your life and live by it.* Follow these first six steps as God's direction for your life; then you can know and live in His peace.

Now let's look back at step six.

Guys Can Really Spout A Line

A guy can be out there spouting a line to a gal while his mama is still doing everything for him at home, including washing his underwear.

You see, God created women to be helpmeets for men, so that as heirs together they can fulfill God's plan for their lives as a couple. But if a guy isn't going anywhere, a woman can't be any help to him.

The way I see it, God created my daughters to be helpmeets for young men who are going somewhere. When a young man isn't going anywhere, he has no vision for his life. So that means he has no need of a wife. He doesn't need help going nowhere; he can do that just fine all by himself.

A guy can really spout a line to a girl, saying things like: "I just love you, Baby. You're the only one for me. I'll follow you all the days of my life. There will never be anyone for me but you."

But words are cheap.

As stated earlier, young people often become too close too soon. They don't need to spend too much time together when they have nothing to do. They can be the ugliest man and the ugliest woman in the world, but if they are put together long enough, something biological will probably happen.

I will give you some illustrations here, then we'll look further into dating.

Functions Of The Physical Body

Thanksgiving is a wonderful time of the year. Let's say you wake up one Thanksgiving morning and you're lying there in bed. Without even opening your eyes, you can tell what day it is. All you have to do is take a whiff of the air. You can smell all the turkey, ham, sweet-potato casserole and apple pie being prepared in the kitchen.

Just by smelling, your mouth starts to release some saliva. Then your stomach releases those amino acids. You haven't as yet seen or tasted any food, but your body is ready for it. You didn't have to intercede for three days or confess it or ask God for your body to get ready to eat; it just happened. That's a God-given function of your physical body.

Using another example, let's say one night you've been helping out at church as a blessing to your pastor. There happened to be a storm that night and, as a result, the electricity is off. Now everyone has gone home, and you're the last person to leave the building. You walk across the parking lot and all the lights are out, so it's dark and the wind is blowing.

While trying to unlock your car door, you have to bend down to see in the dark. Suddenly, someone jumps out from behind the car and cries, "Boo!" At that moment your body releases a shot of adrenalin into your system. You don't have to pray and ask God for it. That's a God-given function of the physical body.

God is so good to give us options, and you have two: either fight or run. You have the energy to do either. God leaves that choice up to you. So you size it up quickly and function accordingly.

A third example would be a boy and a girl who are sitting in a car. They might just be holding hands or they might be passionately kissing. At some point in their relationship, their physical anatomies will release a shot of blood to their sexual organs in anticipation of sexual intercourse. They don't need to jump up and rebuke the devil; he isn't responsible. This is a God-given bodily function.

According to Proverbs 6:27, when there is fire in a man's bosom, even his clothes will be burned. No man can put it out.

These young people have passed a point that they never should have reached to begin with. Maybe they had already been told, "Now always remember, don't do anything to hurt your daddy." But that won't hold water. When they find themselves together like this in the car, it's as if Dad and Mom have moved off to some other planet.

How To Establish A Standard For Courtship

As parents, we will never be able to really hold our children with our own words. The only things that will hold them are God's Word put inside them and the Holy Spirit working together with that Word.

Now, Mom and Dad, let's look at some pointers on how to establish a standard for courtship. My words are not intended as "Thus saith the Lord," but "thus saith Joe McGee." These are based upon my study of God's Word, my years of counseling parents and young people and my experiences as a school administrator and children's pastor.

I can share my own experiences and the standards I have set for my kids that I feel have worked for a lot of other families. But don't use these standards as your own; they won't necessarily work for you. You need to set up your own system using your own standards, based on your convictions of what the Bible says.

Unless you set a standard for your kids, they will have no idea where the boundary line is drawn, so create your own standard for them. They will either love you for it or eventually hate you because you didn't make them do it right.

On more than one occasion in counseling sessions, I have seen young people sit there and scream at their parents for not making them do right. Those are the same kids who at one time were screaming for their parents to give them more freedom. Kids want somebody to tell them what to do. They're saying, "Please show me the right way." But a parent can't be a dictator over them.

In the book *Why Wait? What You Need To Know About The Teen Sexuality Crisis* (San Bernadino, CA: Here's Life Publishers, 1987), Josh McDowell and Dick Day cite research done by two professors – one from Utah State University and another from Brigham Young University – among 2,400 teens, which showed that the younger a girl begins to date, the more likely she is to have sex before graduating from high school. Of girls who began dating at age 12, 91 percent had sex before graduation, compared to 20 percent who began dating at age 16. That isn't even "Thus saith the Lord"; it's just a natural statistic.

But remember this: there is no condemnation and there should be no guilt. That's why we have the blood of Jesus. Nobody is perfect; everybody has sinned – moms, dads and young people. We aren't talking about the past but about the future – our next generation. We, the parents, must pass the wisdom of God on to our children. God has a better way of doing things – much better than the world has taught us.

Set An Age To Begin Dating

Our family standard for dating was a series of steps.

Step # 1: No child was allowed to date before age sixteen.

Again, you need to make up your own set of standards. Take this example of my standard and use it as you choose. Throw out parts of it, slice it, dice it, maybe use a part of it.

Step # 2: When some guy asked one of my daughters for a date, her answer was always the same: "My dad has my social calendar and all my dates are screened through him. I'll be glad to go out with you; you just have to call Dad."

If some guy she didn't want to date asked her out, she had time to get to me. She didn't have to lie, telling him, "Oh, I have lots to do tonight, so I can't possibly go out with you."

> **God has a better way of doing things – much better than the world has taught us.**

On the other hand, if the guy was someone she was interested in, she could run home quickly and say, "Daddy, this neat guy is going to call, and I really want to go out with him. Can you do something quick?"

One thing this did was take the heat off my daughters from guys putting pressure on them.

By requiring them to talk with me first, I eliminated every wimp who would even think about spending time alone with my daughter. If a young man didn't have enough hair on his lip to face a big teddy bear like me, he certainly didn't deserve to spend one-on-one time with my daughter. I have no qualms about that at all. What would he do when out on a date with my daughter if somebody attacked him? Would he turn around and run, leaving my daughter just standing there?

The "First Date" Is With Dad

Step # 3: The "first date" was to be between the young man and me (or her mother).

Once the young man agreed to call and ask for a date with my daughter, he found out that his "first date" was with me. He was required to face me before he would be allowed to date my daughter. I invited him to come over to the house and spend some time with me, or perhaps I could meet him someplace.

I don't mean he could just come by thirty minutes early and visit with me before taking my daughter out on their first date. I intended for him to spend time alone with me. We might eat some pie and drink coffee, play basketball or go to a ball game.

I wanted to get to know a young man before I would allow him to go anywhere with my girl.

The main question I always asked the guy is: "What do you see yourself doing five years from now?" I asked this same question of every boy who wanted to date a daughter of mine. I wanted to know if he was thinking about the future. The purpose of dating is to find a mate. If my daughter's role is to be a helpmeet, she needed to know what she would be helping him to do.

I wanted these boys to be real. I didn't want them just spouting out something that they had memorized; I wanted them to think seriously about what they might do with their lives.

Five Dates With The Family

Step # 4: The next four or five dates would be with the whole family.

If the young man made it past the first date with me, I would permit him to start dating my girl. The next four or five dates were with us as a family. That didn't include going to church, by the way. I can't really get to know a person sitting in a church pew.

These first few dates as a family included doing things together, such as going to ball games. These times allowed me to see a guy act and react. I wanted him to unlock his jaw and let me hear him talk, because out of the abundance of the heart the mouth speaks.

The Double Date

Step # 5: After those four or five dates with the family, then double dates were allowed.

The double date was with a preapproved agenda, which was to be brought to me in writing, and was with another couple, which again I had preapproved. Let me give you an example.

Suppose the young man told me they would be at the pizza restaurant at 9:15 p.m. That means if I picked up the phone at 9:17 p.m., called the restaurant and asked to speak to my daughter, she had better come to the phone.

I expected my daughter to be home by 11:00 p.m., and I expected her date to be at his home by 11:30. In fact, I would call his house to make sure he got there.

"Did your son make it home okay?" I asked.

"Oh, yes, he's here," they'd say. "Thanks, Mr. McGee; we appreciate your calling."

I didn't want that young man to be out running around late at night; he needed to be home. That's why God made the sun go down. After the sun has set, people should be settling in.

A Single Date

Here's the kicker.

Step # 6: Single dates were allowed only after high school graduation.

My daughters were allowed to go on a single date with a guy as soon as they got their high-school diplomas. That's after he had his first date with me, several family dates, and I was given a preapproved agenda, showing where he was taking her on their double dates.

Do you know what happened when they went out on that single date? That young man may have been looking into my daughter's beautiful eyes, but whose face would he see? *Mine!* He couldn't go anywhere without me!

If you will do this, Mom and Dad, you will elevate the value of your daughter in every boy's eyes.

My Daughters Weren't Wallflowers

Some people may say, "I bet your daughters had no social life." But the opposite is true.

My kids were among the most socially active in their schools, and my daughters are beautiful. Thank God, they look like their mother!

We owned a 1986 Ford Aerostar Van which we had bought brand new, and in five years we had put 234,000 miles on it. In December of the following year we bought a Suburban, and in only one year it had 54,000 miles on it. I would call that being more than "socially active." The way we see it: our children are worth it.

Pay Now, Or Pay Later

That's why when we talk to our children, they listen. It's not because we were dictators; we just created a relationship with them. We know them and we are there for them.

As a parent, you either pay now, or you will pay later. You may think you don't have time, but you are going to pay with time somewhere. I would much rather pay it now. You have to set up situations with your kids where they know you and trust you, and you know them.

We are not dictators always following our children around. But we believe in being very involved with their social lives. We like for them to be social. When they are in a social situation, they get to really see the guy they thought was some good-looking hunk. Eventually, he will open his mouth and say something stupid, and they will see it. They will realize, while none of us are perfect, we should be able to recognize the difference between good and evil.

"Dad, You Were Right"

One day when I was out of town, I called home and talked with one of my kids, who said, "Dad, we went out to the ball game with Such-and-such and So-and-so. Do you know what they said? Dad, you were right!"

I don't know how many times I've heard these words: "Gee, Dad, you were right."

One time I remember coming home and hearing, "Dad, So-and-so's going with So-and-so."

My response was: "I give it three months, Honey. I like those kids, but it isn't serious. It's just temporary puppy love. I've been there and I know what I'm talking about."

Sure enough, within two months, they had broken up and I was told, "Dad – you were right."

"Honey," I said, "I didn't come in on the pumpkin wagon. I've been your age before."

I'm Trying To Say Yes

All I want to do is get parents to seek God's wisdom in His Word.

We have to create situations and an atmosphere where our young people can get together. If you say, "I don't know how," then pray and ask God. He will show you. You can't always be saying to your kids, "No! You can't! Don't! Stop!" They will just rebel against that kind of negativity. You have to find positive things that they can do.

I've sat down with each of my children and said to them, "I have predetermined in my mind that every time you ask me for something I'm trying every way I can to say yes."

Before that, I always tried to say no just because that's what I wanted to do. Have you ever done that as a parent? I would say, "No, bless God, you have no business doing that! Why? Because I said so!" That doesn't make much sense, and it won't carry much weight down the road.

So, I've told my kids that I am trying to find a way to say yes every time they ask me something; then when I say something that I mean, it carries much more weight.

As parents we have to teach our children how to pick out friends or they will never know how to pick out a lifetime mate. We have to tell them the truth. If we don't, they will believe the lies they hear from somebody else. Remember that.

CHAPTER 14

Teaching Kids About Sex

The time will come – if it hasn't already – when your child will want to know about sex. You need to realize that he will find out about it from somebody, so it had better be from you. You must be willing to take the time to teach him about sex, but it isn't something you can do in five minutes.

One time at a men's retreat I remember a dad saying to me, "Well, we had the meeting last night."

"What meeting?" I asked.

"With my boy. I talked to him about the birds and the bees."

"Really? Did you get everything said?"

"Oh, yeah, we covered it all."

"Do you think your boy understood it?"

"No problem. It wasn't nearly as hard as I thought it would be. But, thank God, that's over!"

My response to him was: "I guarantee you, Dad, you aren't done; you've just started. You've opened the lid to the box, but nothing has even come out yet."

Children don't need to be reading articles from magazines and the Internet to find out about human sexuality. They need to be talking to men and women of God about it, specifically their parents.

> **God is the one who created sex, but people seem to act as if they think the devil did it.**

God is the one who created sex, but people seem to act as if they think the devil did it. Sometimes I feel that Christians just let their heads go out to lunch on this subject. Most of us as parents don't really know how to talk with our children about sex, primarily because our parents probably didn't talk with us about it or their parents with them. It can be uncomfortable.

Dad says to his son, "Do you know what to do?"

"Oh, yeah, Dad; I know all about it."

"Well, that's good. But you had better not ever do it!"

"Don't worry, Dad."

All I can say is, we parents had better have more to say about the subject than that!

Suppose Mom is standing at the sink doing the dishes and her child asks her a question about sex. She can't be shocked and just drop a plate or pass out right there. She has to keep herself under control in order to handle the situation correctly.

Parents, be careful not to overreact when faced with your child's questions about sex. Just act normal, stay calm and simply answer the question you have been asked.

Make Your Answer Fit The Hearer

If it's your five-year-old asking the question, give an answer a five-year-old can understand. If your ten-year-old asks it, give an answer a ten-year-old can understand. Don't answer your kid the same way you would talk with a twenty-five-year old. It isn't necessary that you go into a five-hour dissertation, using all kinds of graphs and charts. Just tell your kid what he needs to know and let that be all for now.

One year I was attending a Christian conference in Springfield, Missouri. At one of the meetings a professor taught a good session on the subject of teaching our children about sex. He took questions from the audience and just talked with us.

At one point he made this statement: "When talking to your kids about sex, don't make up names for parts of the anatomy, like calling the penis a 'ying-ying' or 'wing-wang.' Call body parts what they are."

That's when a lady stood up and said, "Professor, I have a problem with what you just said."

"What?" he asked.

"I can't say that word."

"What word?"

"The word you just told us to use."

"You mean 'penis'?"

"That's the word!"

"What's your problem, Ma'am?"

"Well, I have a seven-year-old son, and I'm just wondering what I need to do."

"If you don't call it that," he said, "what do you call it?"

"I call it 'his turtle,'" she said.

Her statement brought down the house! It took a moment for the speaker to compose himself and be able to continue with his discussion.

Ignorance About Sex

As a school administrator, I saw many junior-high boys get so embarrassed about sex. You might be shocked at how ignorant most of our kids are. You may think they know everything about it; but they don't really know anything – nobody has ever told them!

I've dealt with young men who are as ignorant as can be about sex because their parents didn't talk to them about it. We read stories all the time about girls who have babies without even knowing they were pregnant; some don't have the slightest idea how they got pregnant.

Now you may think there's no way that could ever happen with so much information available, but it does.

Some girls will say, "Well, I did so-and-so and thought that would keep me from getting pregnant." That's ignorance gone to seed!

Children don't know about sex because their parents haven't talked to them about it.

Why not? Because their parents don't know how.

But it's time we find out how.

God Made Sex To Be Good

Did you know there are references to sex all throughout the Bible?

When I'm talking to parents about teaching their children, the first thing I say to them is: "Don't lie to your kids."

God made sex and He made it to be good. But the devil is working hard against it because it's so precious to God. Don't let the world teach your children and make sex sound perverted. Virginity and the sexual act of marriage were set up by God. The world's system is working against our children, trying to pervert sex every way that it can.

The average age of the onset of puberty in America is much earlier than it was just a century ago, yet the average age for a person to get married is much later than it was a century ago. The gap between the beginning of teens' sexual maturity and the age that they get married, coupled with intense cultural pressure, has many young people desperately looking for close and intimate relationships, leaving them at an extreme risk for sexual sin.

I have a way to combat this: it's called the truth of God's Word.

When talking to parents, I say: "When your kids ask you about sex, don't lie to them. Sit down with them, talk with them and tell them the truth. Tell them that sex is good and that moms and dads love having sex. Tell them that sex is a wonderful part of marriage. But then tell them that because God did not intend for people to have sex outside of marriage, doing so is dangerous and will bring consequences."

If parents will say something like that, it might make their children think before getting themselves into a mess.

> **Don't let the world teach your children and make sex sound perverted.**

Sex Is Like The Ark Of God

In 2 Samuel 6, there is the story of David having the ark of the covenant brought back to Jerusalem. The ark was a very special box that contained the glory, the power and the awesome wonder of Almighty God.

When they were bringing the ark back to Jerusalem. David and the people were dancing and having themselves a joyous time. Then all of a sudden, the ox cart hit a bump in the road and the box began to fall, so a man named Uzzah reached out to stop the box from falling to the ground. But the moment he touched that box, he dropped dead as a doornail! (See 2 Samuel 6:5-7.)

I can imagine how that must have caused everybody to stop their singing and dancing. Standing around, one person asked, "What happened?" Another said, "I don't know – he touched the box and just dropped dead."

At that point David was afraid, so he decided against taking the ark into the city. Consider what happened next: David turned aside to a farmhouse that was owned by a man named Obed-edom the Gittite. Their conversation may have sounded something like this:

The farmer came to the door and said, "Yes? What is it?"

"My name is David. I am the king at Jerusalem. We were coming by, and we have this box here."

Obed-edom asked, "What box?"

"It's God's house. He lives there in that box. I want to know if we can leave it in your living room?"

Obed-edom yelled to his wife, "Martha, come here a minute! Is it okay if they leave that box here with us?"

"Sure. Bring it on in," she said.

Then David gave him a warning: "Whatever you do, don't touch that box. Don't even dust it. We have a problem with it, and we need to figure out what to do."

So Obed-edom said, "Okay. Bring it on in." Then he said, "Now, Martha, don't touch that box. I don't care how dusty it gets."

Verse 11 tells us how the ark was left there for three months. David went on to Jerusalem and tried to find out what went wrong. Then something happened. He got word from Obed-edom, saying, "I want you to come and get that box!"

"What's the problem?"

"Ever since you left it at my place, my sheep, camels and cattle have increased, and the dung is piled up to my eyeballs! Get that box out of here!" (As 2 Samuel 6:12 says, **"The Lord hath blessed the house of Obed-edom, and all that pertaineth unto him, because of the ark of God."**)

The box where God lived was meant to bring blessing, abundant protection and provision. Obed-edom just had it there in his living room. He wasn't praying and asking it to do a thing; he was just watching it. Verse 12 tells how the blessing of God overtook him because of the ark. But that's the same box that caused another man to drop dead.

That's the way I think of sex. Sex was created by God for marriage. It's a wonderful thing, a part of the marriage relationship. But outside of marriage, it can kill you mentally, emotionally, socially and physically.

You see, David figured out why that happened with the box: he didn't read the instructions. God meant for the box to be handled in a certain way, but it wasn't handled the way God had said and, as a result, Uzzah fell dead.

When David went back and read the scroll, one of the instructions said, "Don't touch the box." David thought, *That's an important point. If I had read that, I would have known not to touch the box.*

No Sex Before Marriage

In teaching your children about sex, don't lie to them, but say: "Sex is one of the greatest things that ever happened to the marriage relationship. You're going to love it, but don't mess with it. It was created by God. If you handle it wrong, you could mess up your life."

I tell young people that it's God's will and God's best for them to wait to have sex after marriage and to have sex only with their spouse. Then it will be great. But having sex before marriage will kill them – physically, mentally, and socially – as well as, kill their relationship. It's sin.

When telling that to young people, I can almost see the fear of God come on them – and that's exactly what I want.

Some kids start snickering when talking about sex. But if you've told your kids the truth, they aren't going to be caught up in all those snickers. They know what sex is and what it isn't; and they will come to see it as a part of life.

I highly recommend that you take the time needed to talk to your kids about sex. Maybe you don't know where to start or you don't know all the terminology. There are some great books that you can find in Christian bookstores to help teach your children about it.

Remember, the devil is working on your kids every day, but he is a liar. Don't let your kids be led away by listening to his lies. The way you stop lies is with the truth, and the truth comes first from the Bible and then from knowledgeable books on human sexuality.

There are two great books on this subject which I would recommend: *Sex Education Is For The Family* (Grand Rapids, MI: Zondervan, 1985) by Tim LaHaye and *Why Wait? What You Need To Know About The Teen Sexuality Crisis* (Nashville, TN: Thomas Nelson, 1994) by Josh McDowell and Dick Day.

CHAPTER 15

Marital Conflict

Now the whole idea behind friendship is that eventually people are headed toward the goal of choosing a lifetime mate.

If our kids can't even pick out good friends, how will they ever be able to pick out lifetime mates?

Lots of kids don't have any friends because they are trying so hard to pick out a mate. It's as if they're jumping from square one to square twelve and missing everything in between. But it won't work that way.

The First Sin And Its Consequences

Now I want us to look at what happened in Genesis 3. This isn't a very edifying chapter; it's about what took place in the beginning when God's curses were spoken into existence.

Adam and Eve had just sinned against God's commandments, so they were hiding from Him.

Then God came down and asked where Adam was. Now don't think God didn't know where Adam was; He knew exactly where Adam was. But He wanted Adam to respond.

Finally, Adam said, "I'm here, Lord."

"What are you doing, Adam?"

"I'm hiding."

Then God pressed Adam, asking what the problem was, so Adam said: "It's the wife You gave me, Lord. Everything was going well until You gave her to me. She made me eat some of that fruit – the one You told me not to eat. She did it, Lord, and she's hiding over there. You ought to go talk to her."

So God went over to her and said, "Eve, what happened?"

"Well, Lord, it's like this: Everything was going along really smooth. But You know that snake You made? He came in here and told me a bunch of lies. If You hadn't made that snake, Lord, this never would have happened. He lied to me and tricked me into eating that fruit. It's all his fault!"

God then went over to the serpent and spoke a curse to him, saying: "Serpent, you are cursed above every animal. You are going to crawl on your belly and eat dust the rest of your life."

Then God turned back to Adam and Eve and began telling them what would happen as a result of their sin. He said to them, "Adam, you're going to have to work by the sweat of your brow; and, Eve, you're going to have pain in childbirth." (See Genesis 3:10-19.)

Marital Conflict – A Result Of Sin

I want us to look specifically at Genesis 3:16, where God said to the woman:

...I will greatly multiply thy sorrow and thy conception; in sorrow thou shalt bring forth children; and thy desire shall be to thy husband, and he shall rule over thee.

The last portion of this verse is a strange statement for God to put in with all these curses. Again, he says:

...And thy desire shall be to thy husband, and he shall rule over thee.

God was saying, "By the way, part of the curse in sin is that the wife is going to desire her husband, and he shall rule over her."

This doesn't make much sense when you read it in the King James Version, so let me explain what this part of God's curse really means. Basically, it's saying:

> **Whenever two people get married without Jesus in their lives, they're destined for a rocky marriage.**

"Mister, here's what will happen now that sin is on this planet: You will find a wife, get married and go away on your honeymoon. But then one morning as you're getting ready for work, you'll grab a pair of pants and shove one leg inside them. Then you'll stand up and try to shove your other leg down the other side. But there will be a problem. When shoving your leg down the other side, you'll find that somebody else already has her leg inside those pants. Both you and your wife will be trying to wear the pants in the family!"

A major result of sin is marital conflict. Whenever two people get married without Jesus in their lives, they're destined for a rocky marriage. That is part of the curse which said: "Woman, your husband will rule over you – which means because of the sin nature in you, your desire will be to rule over him" (Genesis 3:16 Author's paraphrase).

God was saying, "Women, your desire will be to rule over your husbands and, men, you shall rule over your wives."

The two clauses of Genesis 3:16 – *Thy desire shall be to thy husband* and *he shall rule over thee* – are in contrast to each other. These are antithetical in the Hebrew sentence structure. Thus, sin destroyed the marriage harmony.

This is where male chauvinism and feminism come from. Instead of submitting to one another in love, each is trying to dominate the other.

Men don't really know how to treat their wives. They want to rule like Attila the Hun, saying, "I'm the biggest and the smartest, so I'm in charge!"

So what we have here is a situation where two people supposedly "feel in love" when actually what they have is a desire for one another's flesh. They seem to enjoy laughing together and going places together, so they get married. Then after being married a while, they start fighting like cats and dogs.

Their marital conflict is the result of their sin nature. They need to be redeemed from that sin nature, and the Redeemer's name is Jesus. They have to ask forgiveness and be covered by His blood. Then they will have power over the sin in their lives.

> So often young people think they've fallen in love when they couldn't spell the word if you gave them all four letters.

Without that, they will never be able to experience a good marriage. I don't care how much they felt in love or how many dates they had in the beginning. It doesn't matter how many roses or boxes of candy he sent to her or how many valentine cards they exchanged. It's impossible for them to have a truly good marriage if they're living without Jesus!

Less than ten percent of households in our country live in a home where the father is the primary breadwinner and the mother stays home with the children. That means the majority of us are living in a different situation, which can create some challenges.

Know The Truth

God loves for males and females to get together. He made it that way for a man and a woman. It was His idea in the beginning.

We must build each other up in our most holy faith, pray in the power of the Holy Spirit, and keep ourselves safe in God's love.

So often, young people think they've fallen in love when they couldn't spell the word if you gave them all four letters. They need to be taught some things about life. But they don't need to learn it from the world; they need to learn it from their moms and dads, who tell them the truth. It's the truth that sets us free and keeps us free (John 8:32).

CHAPTER 16

Lives Committed To God

Sometimes people will look at me say, "Joe, with the number of kids you have, aren't you worried about living in today's times?"

"No, I'm actually excited about all the opportunities. As Psalm 112: 1-2 says, **if I fear the Lord and delight greatly in His commandments, my children will be mighty upon the earth,** and I believe what the Bible says. I know my children can be klutzy sometimes and they can mess up, but they're going to be mighty upon this earth. I didn't just make up that statement. God said it, so I believe it."

"But how are they going to survive, Joe? Dear God, don't you think this economy is bad?"

"Well, as my Bible says, wealth and riches will be in their house, so I don't care what happens to the economy, my children will be blessed" (Psalm 112:3).

Knowing The Good Makes You Recognize The Evil

As mentioned earlier in our study, Daniel and those other boys were taken into captivity by King Nebuchadnezzar. They were made slaves; yet they prospered wonderfully.

Years ago when we took our children to Washington, D.C., we went to the mint and watched money being made. That day they were producing $20 bills, and we saw pallets of those bills lined up there.

Our tour guide told us that in one room FBI agents were being trained to spot counterfeit money. That's their specialty. They go through special training, but not once in the entire program do they see a counterfeit bill. They spend their time studying the good bills; then they will know a counterfeit when they see it.

> **When our children see something evil, they'll say, "That's evil; I can tell just by looking at it."**

I've been some places in this country where people are trying to teach their kids all about the evil in this world. They say, "We have to teach them about things like suicide, drugs and sexual promiscuity and how they are so bad."

When visiting with one youth group, I asked about the films they had been shown, and they said they saw a graphic film on suicide. I don't want my children watching that stuff.

You might say, "We need to teach them about drugs. They have to know how it's done so that they won't do it."

No, they don't!

That's what happened in the Garden of Eden. Adam and Eve knew the goodness of God; they didn't know the evil. But the moment they took the forbidden fruit, they could see the evil. That's when they had to leave the garden.

I'm not saying we should never be teaching our children about pitfalls to avoid, but we have to use wisdom and not fill them up with only what is evil.

Our Children Need To Know God's Word

Our children don't need to be taught the evil; they need to be taught the pure and good Word of God. Then when they see something evil, they'll say, "That's evil; I can tell just by looking at it." Why? "Not because I have studied evil, but because I know what good is." We want them to know the good.

Our children need to know that God's vision for them is good for all of their lives. They may say: "But God won't do anything for me. I'll be poor and ugly and probably marry an ugly person because God wants me to. Besides, all the good ones are getting married off, so there won't be anyone I would want left for me!"

That's a lie! God said He would give us the desires of our hearts (Psalm 37:4). God has good plans for us. But if we don't read His Book, we won't know that. He says He will do above and beyond all we ask or think (Ephesians 3:20). Jesus wants to be Lord over our social lives just as much as any other area.

Remember, if Jesus tarries, we parents must be teaching our next generation about the church and about the principles of God's Word. Our children must then go on to do more than we have done – and they will.

We Must Develop The Life Of Jesus In Our Kids

Our job is simple. All we have to do is develop within our kids the four things Jesus developed in His life here on earth.

First, we must plant God's *vision* inside them.

Second, we must see that they become *self-disciplined*.

Third, we must teach them that they aren't stupid, but they are *gifted to succeed* in this life here on earth.

Fourth, we must teach them the value of true *friendship* – how to be a true friend to others, how to have others be true to them in their relationships throughout life, and how to get along with both friends and enemies.

Perfection In This Life Is A Myth

As I've told my children: "My love and God's love for you are not based on whether you are a straight-A student or you make the basketball team. We love you just as you are. Success will come to you if you stay diligent because God has put within you the ability to succeed, and you will be successful in some area of life."

The world acts like perfection is for everybody and it constantly paints a picture of perfection. Every advertisement on TV shows people around the house dressed up as if they're headed for church. You never see a commercial for dish soap in a dirty house. They work hard at presenting a false picture of perfection.

But we aren't perfect. We are righteous. We are forgiven. We will fall down at times, but we are to get back up again (Proverbs 24:16).

When we keep getting up, it frustrates the devil to no end. He says, "I thought I knocked them down, but they're standing up again!" He keeps trying to mess us up and is always wanting us to feel guilty.

But I say to him: "There is no condemnation to those who are in Christ Jesus, and I happen to be in Christ Jesus right now. So, devil, you have to take it up with Him!" (Romans 8:1)

Then I get up again and keep moving. I want my children to do that, too.

"What happened, Son?"

"I fell down, Dad."

"That's all right, Son. Just get back up again. Let's repent to God, get our hands back on the plow and get moving again."

This applies to children in every area of their lives, whether on the basketball court, in academics, in relationships with their parents and friends, or just life in general.

God isn't saying to anyone, "You deserve to fall down; you've been sinning." God never says that to anybody who has sinned. He keeps saying, "Repent and get up. I'm not mad at you. I have never been mad at you and never will be; I love you. So repent, get up and go on with life."

> God isn't saying to anyone, "You deserve to fall down." He keeps saying, "Repent and get up. I'm not mad at you."

It's important that we live this same way toward our children.

Be The Number-One Cheerleader

We have to be the number-one cheerleader in our homes. You can be, and I believe you will be.

If you've read all the way through this book, perhaps you've learned more about your job as a parent. Let me tell you what I think you need to do now.

These days we've heard plenty of truth being preached in our good churches. What God wants us to do now is to act on what we know. We have to be a living example to other people, especially to our children, of what God says in His Word. Sometimes it's good for us to confess boldly before others that Jesus is the Lord and Savior of our lives.

Now I want to give you the opportunity to make an outward show of commitment to God. If you are willing to do so, pray this:

> *Father, in the name of Jesus, I come to You and I confess that, as a parent, I realize I can do nothing without Jesus, but that with Him all things are possible.*
>
> *The enemy has come as the accuser of the brethren to make me feel guilty for doing things I should not have done and for failing to do the things I should have done as a parent. He has tried to make me feel guilty for saying things to my children I should not have said and for failing to say the things I could have said.*
>
> *I ask You now, in accordance with 1 John 1:9, to forgive me of any sins I have committed against You, against my family, against my fellow man or even against my own flesh. I thank You for washing me clean by the blood of Jesus, and for taking my sins from me as far as the east is from the west.*
>
> *I refuse to let the devil hold me in the past any longer.*
>
> *Father, give me wisdom as a parent to train up my child in the way he should go.*
>
> *For my child, I ask three things:*
>
> **First: Teach my child to fear You!**
>
> *Psalm 34:11 – **Come, ye children, hearken unto me: I will teach you the fear of the Lord.***
>
> *Proverbs 9:10 – **The fear of the Lord is the beginning of wisdom.…***
>
> *Proverbs 3:16 – **Length of days is in her (wisdom's) right hand; and in her left hand riches and honour.***
>
> *As it says in Your Word, the fear of the Lord is the beginning of wisdom, and with wisdom will come long life, wealth, riches and honor to my child.*

Second: Surround my child with the shield of divine favor.

*Psalm 5:12 – **For thou, Lord, wilt bless the righteous; with favour wilt thou compass him as with a shield.***

*John 16:33 – Jesus said, ... **In the world ye shall have tribulation: but be of good cheer; I have overcome the world.***

*Luke 6:28 – **Bless them that curse you, and pray for them which despitefully use you.***

In the world there are those who would want to use or abuse my children, so help my children to do righteously and surround them with a shield of divine favor. Just as Joseph and Daniel were in captivity – with the wrong culture, wrong language, wrong religion; having no friends, no family, no finances, no influence – they both ended up running the very countries that took them captive. May my children know your favor.

Third: Send godly friends into my children's lives who will sharpen them like iron and cause them to be all You want them to be.

*Proverbs 27:17 NIV – **As iron sharpens iron, so one person sharpens another.***

*Proverbs 13:20 – **He that walketh with wise men shall be wise: but a companion of fools shall be destroyed.***

*Proverbs 14:7 – **Go from the presence of a foolish man, when thou perceivest not in him the lips of knowledge.***

Father, there are more than 100 scriptures in the Word of God relating to friends and friendship. I know how important friendships are to my children, so I thank You now for bringing godly friends into their lives.

I pray these three things for my kids in Jesus' name, and I give You all the praise, honor and glory for bringing it to pass in their lives. Amen.

Conclusion

Much could have been written here that wasn't. I certainly did not exhaust the subject of parenting. I could have given dozens more scriptures and illustrations in this book. But the point has been made: God has the answers.

You see, there are no perfect parents, and I certainly don't consider myself an expert on parenting. My kids will quickly back up this fact. But that's okay since perfection is not a prerequisite for having children.

My goal has been to put hope back into the lives of moms and dads, so I leave you with two thoughts:

1. You cannot do anything about the past except to repent. Once that's done, then it's time to start growing in the grace and knowledge of our Lord Jesus Christ. We are going to be doers of the Word. If we fall, we have to get back up. **"All things are possible to him that believeth"** (Mark 9:23).

2. Biblical parenting does not come about by the changes we force on our children, but by the changes we allow God to make in us. **"A child when fully taught will be just like his teacher"** (Luke 6:40).

God bless your family as you grow in Him.

Prayer For Salvation

If you've never asked Jesus Christ to come into your heart, or you want to rededicate your life to Him – here is a simple prayer you can pray right now to do that.

Those who call on the name of the Lord shall be saved. God does the saving; He just needs your permission.

Dear Heavenly Father,

You said in Your Word, "... If thou shalt confess with thy mouth the Lord Jesus, and shalt believe in thine heart that God hath raised him from the dead, THOU SHALT BE SAVED. For whosoever shall call upon the name of the Lord shall be saved" (Romans 10:9, 13).

According to Your Word, I believe in my heart that Jesus Christ is the Son of God, and I believe He was raised from the dead. I am calling upon His Name – the Name of Jesus – so I know, Father God, that I am now saved.

Your Word says, "... With the heart man believeth unto righteousness; and with the mouth confession is made unto salvation" (Romans 10:10).

I believe with my heart and confess with my mouth Jesus is now my Lord. I am saved. Thank you, Father!

Now That I Am Saved:

1. **Find a good church that teaches the Bible.**

   And let us not neglect our meeting together, as some people do, but encourage one another, especially now that the day of his return is drawing near.

   Hebrews 10:25 NLT

All Scripture is inspired by God and is useful to teach us what is true and to make us realize what is wrong in our lives. It corrects us when we are wrong and teaches us to do what is right.

2 Timothy 3:16 NLT

2. **Buy a good Bible and read it regularly.**

As newborn babes, desire the sincere milk of the word, that you may grow thereby.

1 Peter 2:2

And do not be conformed to this world: but be ye transformed by the renewing of your mind, that you may prove what is that good, and acceptable, and perfect, will of God.

Romans 12:2

3. **Talk to God in prayer.**

Pray without ceasing.

1 Thessalonians 5:17

Be careful for nothing; but in every thing by prayer and supplication with thanksgiving let your requests be made known unto God.

And the peace of God, which passeth all understanding, shall keep your hearts and minds through Christ Jesus.

Philippians 4:6-7

4. **Be baptized.**

Therefore go and make disciples of all the nations, baptizing them in the name of the Father and the Son and the Holy Spirit.

Matthew 28:19 NLT

Then Peter said unto them, Repent, and be baptized every one of you in the name of Jesus Christ for the remission of sins, and ye shall receive the gift of the Holy Ghost.

Acts 2:38

5. Make Christian friends.

The godly give good advice to their friends; the wicked lead them astray.

Proverbs 12:26 NLT

As iron sharpens iron, so a friend sharpens a friend.

Proverbs 27:17 NLT

MEET JOE McGEE

Joe McGee, author, conference speaker and former school administrator shares his laugh-and-learn approach to family relationships across 50 cities annually.

As a husband of more than 40 years and father of 6 grown children, Joe has invested the past 30 years in training people from all walks of life in family, marriage and parenting relationships.

His laugh-and-learn approach removes barriers and provides a refreshing point of view, a new hope for better families and a deeper commitment to obey God's Word.

Joe and his wife Denise make their home in Tulsa, Oklahoma.

To contact the author or to obtain information on hosting Joe McGee at your church,

Please Contact:

Joe McGee Ministries

P O Box 691498

Tulsa, OK 74169-1498

800-482-5862

www.joemcgeeministries.com

Please include your comments about this book when you write. Prayer requests are welcome.

RESOURCES BY JOE MCGEE

Parenting

Biblical Parenting 101
8 Things No Kid Should Leave Home Without
Parenting Teens
Training And Controlling Your Children
The Single Parent
Raising Happy Kids
Blended Families
Leadership: Homegrown
Smart Moms

Marriage

Marriage Building 101
Caution: Marriage In Progress
Married Beyond Recognition
The Field Guide To Marriage
Before Saying I Do
100 Ways To Love Your Spouse
Man: Lover, Leader, Provider
Of Course I Love You

Success For Everyday

The Importance Of Vision
Foundations For Living
Honey, Don't Panic
Family Finances

For more, visit www.joemcgeestore.com

Scan the QR code to visit Joe's Store online.

For Free Resources And
Joe's Newsletter:

Keep up to date with all our resources and information, and check out Joe McGee's online newsletter at joemcgeeministries.com.

Joe's Recommended Reading List

For more information about this topic or other related materials, check out Joe McGee's recommended reading list at joemcgeeministries.com.

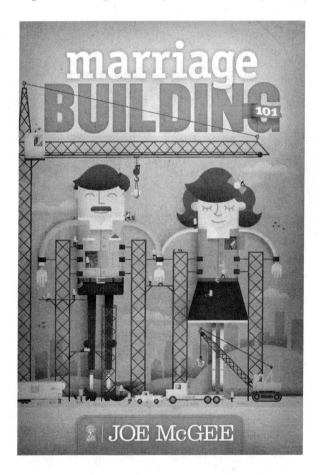

I've Got Children, Now What?

None of us became parents because we were the most qualified, but God has us covered.

In Biblical Parenting 101 discover the four principles of raising children.

Biblical Parenting 101

Available on CD or DVD

Prepare Your Child For A Great Future!

"Take heed to *8 Things No Kid Should Leave Home Without.* This one is to be read and re-read as a manual for making disciples of those we must reach first – our own kids!"
– Pastor Willie George, Church on the Move, Tulsa, OK

8 Things No Kid Should Leave Home Without

Book and CD

Needing Direction In Your Life?

The Importance of Vision

Available on CD

Know Prayer, Know Power

Available on CD

Visit www.joemcgeeministries.com or call 800-482-5862 to order!